ENDO

WOW—I'm not sure what else to say. I couldn't put this book down once I started reading. It is written in the "heavenly language of faith"—with every chapter, I could literally feel faith fill me. This book is created to be a classic; it is a must-read and should be in everyone's personal library. Thank you, Donna Schambach, for this wonderful treasure!

PATRICIA KING
Founder, Patricia King Ministries
patriciaking.com

Evangelist R. W. Schambach was used powerfully by God to build bold faith into the hearts of believers to experience miracles. In *The Anointing for Miracles*, Schambach's daughter, Donna, observes that powerful anointing on her father's life and expresses "keys" for every believer to operate in a supernatural anointing.

MARK BATTERSON
Lead Pastor, National Community Church
New York Times best-selling author of *The Circle Maker*

Donna Schambach has been a friend for lots of years. Her parents were great and so is she. Donna has always followed God and listened to His voice. *The Anointing for Miracles* will bless multitudes. I salute her for writing it.

DODIE OSTEEN
Cofounder of Lakewood Church
Houston, Texas

I work with young adults in a collegiate setting. College students long to experience the mystery and majesty of God's presence and power as displayed in His genuine signs and wonders. They are tired of the hype of commercialized religion. They want to see compassionate, humble servants of God who are not afraid to wade into a crowd of the lost, the sick, the addicted, and the impoverished to show them the love of Jesus. They desire the authenticity and simplicity of those who, with childlike faith, trust Christ to save, heal, deliver, and provide. *The Anointing for Miracles* by R. W. Schambach and Donna Schambach is the book for them! The inspiring Bible-based, step-by-step teachings and firsthand testimonies contained in the pages of this book will build your faith and motivate you to partner with God's supernatural power.

DAVID ARNETT, D.MIN.
President
Northpoint Bible College & Graduate School

R. W. Schambach was an unwavering and unapologetic warrior for truth throughout his entire lifetime of Christian service. His ministry was marked by his willingness to go where others feared to tread—into the cities and neighborhoods where the needs were most urgent and where miracles were manifested in unprecedented measure. His daring faith in the ability of God to demonstrate His power in remarkable ways was rewarded by outpourings of miracles that rival those of any age of human history. I am thrilled that Donna Schambach, Brother Schambach's daughter and an anointed evangelist as well, has chosen to add her unique insights and to release her father's book to a new generation of believers. You will be uplifted, inspired, and encouraged by *The Anointing for Miracles*.

ROD PARSLEY
Pastor, World Harvest Church
Columbus, Ohio

Schambach. It's not a common name, and he was no common man. Sure, R. W. Schambach would use those cowboy boots to squash any suggestion that he was special. But anyone who saw him or heard him on the radio, knew that his anointing was as unique as his name, Schambach. Like "Wigglesworth," another odd name, Brother Schambach understood the grit of shavings and raw living, yet also the fragrance of oil and sweet anointing.

Ours is the God of Abraham and Isaac and Jacob. Whatever He wills to do in our lives is always bigger than our lives, and requires another generation to complete. Our family has ministered with Donna Schambach in Latin America and Africa. We've heard the Gospel she preaches. We've seen the miracles that follow. There is no doubt that the anointing still flows in that uncommon name, Schambach. She faithfully walks in the oily footprints left behind by her adoring father. And yet, obedience requires her to step into places and to engage peoples her father might have never imagined. Take this uncommon book and inhale its power and perfume. And as you read its pages, choose to become that next generation who exhales to your own world, "You don't have any trouble. All you need is faith in God!"

Dr. Paul Lanier, Bishop
Hope Community Church
Winston-Salem, North Carolina

Pastor Donna Schambach's eyewitness accounts of the miraculous, throughout her father's ministry and her own, rev the soul of every believer hungry for a fresh move of God. She passionately articulates Abba's fullest intentions for His children. That same God with that same power longs to release that same glory through the life of every Christian. Pastor Schambach awakens the deepest parts of us to believe once again: God Is. God Can. God Does. God Will.

Dr. Debbie Lanier, Pastor
Hope Community Church
Winston-Salem, North Carolina

The Anointing for Miracles is a faith-building book, filled with miracles that R. W. Schambach saw through the power of God going through His hands. I know what it is like to watch God move through my parents, The Happy Hunters, Charles and Frances Hunter. I hear testimonies of healing wherever I go. I never get tired of hearing them. In this book there is the power to ignite you to be used of God in a mighty way. This book will build your faith like nothing before. It will build your faith to see more miracles with your own eyes. Enjoy.

Joan Hunter
Author and Healing Evangelist
www.joanhunter.org.

The memory of R. W. Schambach is faith-building and inspiring to me. My father, Reverend H. R. Bagwell, knew Brother Schambach very well and spoke highly of his anointing and godly character. I recall viewing an old black and white video of my father and Brother Schambach helping Reverend A. A. Allen as they prayed for the sick together. How I wish I could have been there to experience that historical moment!

I was honored to preach under Brother Schambach's great Gospel tent, host him in our church in Denver, and, shortly before his passing, to be with him at the Prophetic Conference at his headquarters in Tyler, Texas. I sat in the audience that day in Tyler listening to the words of this great patriarch and realized how enriched my life was to have known him personally. At that moment, as I was being impacted by his words, I didn't know those would be his final days.

R. W. Schambach truly was a man who walked in great humility, but also in supernatural Holy Spirit power. The world is a better place and the kingdom of God has been strengthened because of his surrendered life. This great book, *The Anointing for Miracles*, is a must-read for people who desire to grow in their walk of faith. The true accounts of miracles and deliverances will be priceless to believers who hunger to have the manifestation of the power of God in their own lives.

Brother Schambach's daughter, Donna, has articulately conveyed revelation of powerful spiritual truths and practical steps on how the believer can function in the gifts of the Holy Spirit. What a marvelous day we live in that the words and revelations of these great men of faith, who have gone on to be with the Lord, can now be transferred to another generation. This book does just that and adds the insight of Donna Schambach who witnessed these amazing spiritual events.

Evangelist Donna Schambach is continuing to carry on the legacy of her world-renowned father. Her heart for the lost and for people worldwide passionately motivates her to continue preaching an uncompromised Gospel. I believe this book will be one you will read over and over again, as it will elevate your faith each time.

Dr. Tim Bagwell, Senior pastor
Word of Life Christian Center
Lone Tree, Colorado

The Anointing for Miracles is a book that had to be written. But more importantly, it is a book that must be read if you are interested not only in the history of the healing revivals, but if you are interested in the anointing of the Holy Spirit upon a life. What was the secret of the success of this famous evangelist? This author knows the answer to that question because as his daughter, she was the one person in the world who knew him best.

I first met my friend Bob Schambach at Central Bible College in Springfield, Missouri. We walked the same halls, sat in the same classrooms, ate in the same cafeteria, attended the same chapel services. At CBI, we sat under the leadership of the late W. I. Evans, who made that school truly a school of the Holy Spirit. Brother Evans taught us, showed us, and demonstrated to us what the anointing of the Holy Spirit meant, and Bob Schambach heard him. He comprehended what this man was talking about. He left that school not only with a great Bible School education but with a seed of hunger for the anointing of God upon his life and ministry. I watched that anointing develop and grow.

Both of us chose the same type of ministry and were part of a group of evangelists who published the *Voice of Healing* magazine. I chose to work with my father in great healing crusades. Bob Schambach chose to work with one of the world's leading healing evangelists, A. A. Allen. I remember visiting one of their healing crusades in Dallas, Texas. We talked for hours at those meetings about Brother Allen's ministry and his anointing. Not only did he observe and eventually share the evangelist's anointing, but he was the most loyal disciple of a man of God I have ever known.

In this book, his daughter, Donna, shares the life of her father as no one in the world can possibly share the story. Not only is Donna a daughter, she is a disciple of her dad and carries the legacy of that same anointing. She not only has accurate knowledge of her father's life but she has walked beside him in ministry and knows what made him the great man he was. If you are hungry for God, if you want to know what happens when the Holy Spirit anoints a life, this book is a must for you. You will not be able to put it down when you start reading. Yes, it is well-written, yes, it is factual; but most of all, it is the intimate story of one of the greatest men who has ever graced this planet from a loving daughter. This book will place a hunger in your heart for God and for His anointing.

I remember one of the last times I worked with Bob Schambach at a telethon for the TCT network. I arrived at the beautiful studio before he arrived. Everything was normal for a telethon. The lights went on, the telethon began, and we all were standing in front of the cameras as our host, Garth Coonce, opened the program. We knew that we would be in that room in front of the cameras for several hours. Then a figure walked through the door and Evangelist Bob Schambach joined us. It was a moment that I will never forget. When that man of God walked onto that set, everything changed. There were other well-known people in that studio. But when Bob arrived, it was as if God had arrived, and in truth, He had.

That night I am sure was successful in providing funding for the network. But most of all I saw the anointing on a man of God that filled a room that filled the homes of thousands who watched that telethon. With the anointing of the Holy Spirit, he was bigger than life. That was my friend, Bob Schambach; he filled great tents, he filled huge auditoriums, but most of all he filled them not just with crowds, but with the presence of God. Like the great prophet of God in the Old Testament as he led the children of Israel to the Promised Land, I would say to Bob Schambach and to readers, "God, if we cannot take the presence of God that was upon this man of God with us, we don't want to go."

You must read this story, but you must look not only for the life story of one of the world's greatest evangelists, but the story of the Holy Spirit. Thank you, Donna, for sharing the story with us.

I believe that thousands will join me in reading a book that will change lives—we will never be the same.

BISHOP TOMMY REID
The Tabernacle
Orchard Park, New York

The legacy of R. W. Schambach and his Christ-centered, anointed, and far-reaching ministry is embodied in the life and ministry of his daughter, Donna. While impacting the masses, bringing healing and deliverance, she does not overlook the individual. Her passion is to help people know Jesus Christ and experience His miracle power. Through this book, you will hear the voice of the great man R. W. Schambach, and you will receive the systematic teaching that produces miracles through the pen of Donna. Together, they bring to you the anointing for miracles. Expect nothing less in your life.

LaDONNA OSBORN, D.MIN.
President and CEO, Osborn Ministries International
Tulsa, Oklahoma

The Anointing for
MIRACLES

The Anointing for
MIRACLES

How to Partner with

GOD'S SUPERNATURAL POWER

R.W. Schambach & Donna J. Schambach

DESTINY IMAGE® PUBLISHERS, INC.
P.O. Box 310
Shippensburg, PA 17257-0310
"Promoting Inspired Lives"

This book and all other Destiny Image and Destiny Image Fiction books are available at Christian bookstores and distributors worldwide.

For more information on foreign distributors, call 717-532-3040.

Or reach us on the Internet: www.destinyimage.com

ISBN 13: 978-0-7684-1053-2
ISBN Ebook: 978-0-7684-1054-9

For Worldwide Distribution, Printed in the U.S.A.
4 5 6 / 20 19 18 17 16

Miracles Previous ISBN 0-89274-811-7
Copyright © 1993 by R. W. Schambach

Miracles 2: Greater Miracles
Previous ISBN 1-888361-52-2
Copyright © 2003 by R. W. Schambach

Miracles Previous ISBN 978-0-7684-2830-8
Copyright © 2006 by R. W. Schambach

CONTENTS

Foreword *by Dr. Mark Chironna* 15

Preface 17

Prologue   "Man's Life Spared from Electric Chair" 23

Chapter 1   The Keys to Partnering with God 27

Chapter 2   Key #1: Faith. 31

Chapter 3   Faith-Building Miracle Stories
                by R. W. Schambach. 41

Chapter 4   Key #2: Holy Spirit Empowerment 51

Chapter 5   Holy Ghost Miracle Stories
                by R. W. Schambach. 59

Chapter 6   Key #3: Compassion 67

Chapter 7   Compassion-Driven Miracle Stories
                by R. W. Schambach. 79

Chapter 8   Key #4: Authority. 87

Chapter 9   Miracles of Authority *by R. W. Schambach*. 99

Chapter 10   Key #5: Obedience 109

Chapter 11   Miracles Requiring Great Obedience
                by R. W. Schambach. 113

Chapter 12   Key #6: Coveting 127

Chapter 13   The Coveting Kind of Faith Miracle Stories
                by R. W. Schambach. 137

Chapter 14   Key #7: Spiritual Perception 155

Chapter 15   Miracle Stories of Holy Spirit Direction
               by R. W. Schambach. 167

Chapter 16   Key #8: Consecration and Holiness 175

Epilogue   A Word from Donna's Mother. 183

               A Word from R. W. Schambach 185

Appendix   More Miracle Testimonies
               by R. W. Schambach 189

               A Blood Transfusion from Calvary. 189

               Miracle Candy 190

               A Miracle in Progress. 193

               My Battle with the Devil 195

               It's Never Too Late. 196

               Twenty-Six Miracles. 198

               Cow Money 204

               Tithing Eggs. 207

               Multiplying Money. 210

               The Miracle of Giving 211

               End-Word
               from Evangelist Donna Schambach 215

FOREWORD

꽃

Dr. Mark J. Chironna

One of the greatest privileges of my faith journey was to ultimately get to know and be befriended by R. W. Schambach. To me personally, he was a hero and a mentor. When I was first converted, I listened to him every day on the radio at 2:30 p.m. driving in my car. I was a college grad, working in the New York City School System, and attending a theological training institute four days a week (all at the same time), in preparation for ministry.

By the time I was to take homiletics, the teachers felt I was not "preaching material" and so recommended I not take the course. I was devastated. Something in my heart, however, knew I was called to preach. I felt a strong impression to continue to listen to my favorite preacher every day and learn by listening! That preacher was R. W. Schambach. I didn't just learn the basics of homiletics, "State, Illustrate, Apply," I learned about walking and speaking in and by faith, understanding spiritual warfare, praying with all manner of prayer, stewardship, and the demonstration of the Spirit and power in signs, wonders, and miracles.

I didn't stop at just listening. I had to go under the "big Gospel tent" when he was in the New York area to hear and see the man close up. If I heard it once, I heard him say a thousand times, "You don't have any trouble, all you need is faith in God!" Brother Schambach mentored me when he had no idea who I was. Years later when we finally had the chance to be on the same platform, it was the greatest honor for me to meet him.

Yet, to get to know him personally was one of the richest rewards of my journey in Christ. I had no idea at the time that Brother Schambach had a daughter, and one night on a major national platform I pulled him aside and said something to the effect that his daughter was his heir-apparent and the carrier of his legacy. It wasn't all that long after that when I met Donna while her dad was ministering for us at our local church in Orlando. The Schambach family has been near and dear to my heart for many years now.

The book you hold in your hands, *The Anointing for Miracles*, is a gem, and the best of the generations in the Schambach family. You'll read and feel the anointing of Brother Schambach in his writing, and you will seamlessly experience that same anointing in his daughter, Donna. What a treasure this is! Don't just read it once, read it again and again, and let the truths contained herein change your life the way they have changed mine. And remember, "You don't have any trouble, all you need is faith in God!"

Dr. Mark J. Chironna
Mark Chironna Ministries
Church On The Living Edge
Orlando, Florida

PREFACE

Donna Schambach

Avisible radiance overshadowed him as he boldly walked onto the platform under the great Gospel tent. He often led with a song, releasing faith into the air as he navigated the manifest presence of God. Within seconds of his stepping into place, something dramatically changed in the atmosphere.

Pacing like a lion stalking his prey, my father, R. W. Schambach, went face to face with demonic spirits, attacking the works of the devil that ravaged lives.

The great canvas cathedral was his domain. As he carefully studied the vast audience, evaluating what he would confront that night, Dad watched and listened for the movement of the Holy Spirit, assessing what God wanted to accomplish in the next moments.

Those of us who knew him recognized the moment his countenance visibly changed. Brother Schambach operated in a laser-focused seriousness that lasted until everyone under the tent heard him preach the Gospel of Jesus Christ. He would offer every heart an opportunity to make a public declaration of faith, repent of their sins, and receive God's healing touch in their physical bodies. We always knew, no matter how much we encouraged him to cut short the services, we would usually be in for a very long night.

We memorized his messages; we had learned his familiar stories; we knew the punch lines of all his jokes—yet, we were always excited, anticipating what God would do uniquely on any particular night when he preached the Gospel.

My favorite times were the altar calls. Whether we were in Philadelphia, Camden, Chicago, or the Bronx—we knew many were present who needed Jesus as Savior. At just the right time, Dad initiated his 30-second "countdown to eternity." During those 30 seconds, he clearly described the benefits of choosing Jesus and the fearful consequences of serving the devil.

"Waaaaaah-one!" His high-pitched voice was loud and strong. "Where will you spend eternity? It's either Heaven or hell, sink or swim, Christ or the devil—it's up to you. You'll either make Heaven your eternal home, or split hell wide open. The choice is yours. Here comes the second one…

"Two-oooh! You'd better get your hand ready. I'm only gonna count one more time. Your heart may be thumping out of your chest. You know you're a sinner. Don't let anyone or the devil lie to you; tomorrow is not promised to you. Are you ready? This is it. Get ready to throw your hands in the air…here it comes…

"Thaaareeee! Shoot those hands up, all over this place."

The truth is, before he actually got to "three" most of the hands were already in the air and people began to file down to the front of the tent. The conviction of the Holy Spirit was real.

I had the privilege of being on the platform at those moments. I watched men, women, boys and girls, teenagers, and elderly folks come to the altar with tears streaming down their faces. Some would kneel; many would weep. The sight was something I could never contain. Usually I was weeping before the first stanza of "There's Room at the Cross" was sung.

We all prayed the sinner's prayer together, every single night—praying it out loud, as though we were praying for a friend or loved one without Christ. Personally, I always felt as though I was getting a fresh cleansing in my heart every night. Dad would pray a line of the prayer and then thousands in front of him and everyone on the platform, repeated after him:

> *Father. In the name of Jesus, I come to You tonight. I come as a sinner. I invite You to come into my heart. Walk in me. Talk in me. Be my God, and I will be Your child. Lord, I admit to You I am so weak. I cannot live this Christian life without You. Wash me in Your blood and fill me with the Holy Ghost. Thank You, Lord, for hearing my prayer. For the rest of my life I will serve only You. I believe on You, Jesus. Right now, I confess, I am born again!*

Dad took his time with the people, encouraging them to read their Bibles every day and pray. He talked to them about a power-relationship with the Holy Spirit and he urged each one to find a good Bible-believing church. Then he gave them their first instructions as new believers: he sent them to our "prayer tent" where a minister, usually my mother's sister Helen, was waiting to give them literature and pray with them.

Every moment up until that point was a kind of "school of the Spirit" on evangelism, but what would happen next was a separate course on the *supernatural and miracles*.

It was different each night. Sometimes Dad sensed to call for cancer victims first. Often he began by praying for those with deaf ears. He looked for some way to encourage the faith of the people by putting the power of God on display. When someone jumped out of a wheelchair or started screaming because they could hear for the first time in their lives, the faith of the crowd soared. People came from every section of the tent to stand in line so Dad could lay his hands on them.

Many were the times—too many to count—when I stood by his side. I watched people jump and sway as though struck by lightning bolts; I saw them tremble and shake themselves all the way to the ground. Some fell like so many cords of wood, out cold for the remainder of the night. Others jumped up and down for the entire length of the ramp; and still others began to run around the tent as though they were outrunning a train.

The power of God was so strong, many who stood by Dad's side, including me, often felt as though we would fall too. Heaven would come to rest on the platform and everyone on it.

We heard wonderful testimonies of God's power each night as many returned to tell of their healing or deliverance. Multitudes through the years were completely set free from alcoholism and drug addiction.

Those amazing tent meetings were wonderfully familiar to me. Even so, I believe too many times I took that atmosphere for granted. Now that Dad is gone and I am ministering on my own, I wish I had been more in tune with what God was doing in every one of those historic services.

You see, Papa was an ordinary, down-to-earth man. He was not one to be arrogant. He walked humbly before God and people. He was gentle of heart with a huge capacity to love. We never introduced him to his audiences as "God's man of faith and power." He would have none of that. He was always, as he put it, "plain ole Brother Schambach."

What set him apart, what deepened his resolve to whip the devil, what gave him a boldness to confront the demon hordes—was *the anointing* of the Holy Spirit. The Holy Spirit Himself poured upon my father a steady stream of holy "oil." He was set apart with Holy Ghost power to preach God's word, "fish" for men, impart faith, and see miracles!

R. W. Schambach was called to a specific time and place for ministry, and he was anointed for that role because of his spiritual hunger and his relationship with the Holy Spirit. He went after miracles with his whole heart. He also instinctively knew the job God wanted to do on the earth was far beyond him. He envisioned entire stadiums filled with seekers hungry for a move of God. According to the last decades of his preaching, he believed God would use him to "raise up an army of believers to do the works of Christ in the character and power of Christ."

Often I heard him proclaim, "The day of the big preacher is over. God is raising up an army to get the job done!" He knew what it took to get the job done—the power of the Holy Spirit. Every book he signed was inscribed: *You shall receive power after that the Holy Ghost shall come upon you. Acts 1:8*

Dad encouraged people to get busy healing the sick and casting out devils, and he was *thrilled* when someone took God at His word by faith and began to do exactly as Jesus instructed! He was the biggest cheerleader of those who sought after and functioned in the anointing for miracles, because he believed demonstrating the Gospel was the best way to convince unbelievers that Jesus is alive and doing the same things He did 2,000 years ago.

In the following chapters of this book, you will read some of the most powerful miracle stories of my father's 60-plus years of ministry. These are stories he told over and over again. Every one of them is a miracle; every one of them will build your faith. Each happened in an ordinary life that dared to trust God.

You will also read the observations of a daughter who apprenticed alongside her father. In my thirty or more years of ministry, I have learned there are distinctions about each individual God uses; and, there are common practices that develop a fuller understanding of faith and the anointing for supernatural works.

As you read this book, I pray you will learn from an ordinary man whom God mightily used. I know you will see some of your own strengths and weaknesses in these accounts; and, I believe, you will begin to operate in a new dimension of revelation and faith as you are obedient to the call on your life.

Go with me now, to a service already in progress...

"MAN'S LIFE SPARED FROM ELECTRIC CHAIR"

Donna Schambach

He was preaching in Newark, New Jersey, in 1960. The time: 9:30 p.m. A woman came walking down the center aisle, and my father, R. W. Schambach, knew what that meant. It meant someone was going to interrupt his message. She walked down the center aisle and stood right in front of the preacher that night. He had his Bible in hand and was preaching a masterpiece! How dare anybody interrupt a man of God?

Actually, that precious woman was interrupting him with the desperate kind of faith, just as four men tore the roof off the place where Jesus was teaching so their friend could get a miracle. Their faith moved the Lord, and that's what real faith does.

When that woman in Newark approached my father, she said, "Brother Schambach, please forgive me. I have never stopped a preacher in my lifetime. But this is an emergency. My son is going to die in the electric chair at ten o'clock."

By his own confession Brother Schambach thought, "Oh, my God!" She knocked the preach right out of him. When he heard that, he couldn't preach another word.

He had prayed for people dying in hospitals, but he had never prayed for anybody who was going to die in the electric chair. This man had been convicted by a jury of his peers. He had been found guilty. He was going to die in order to pay for the murder they said he committed—and it was going to happen in thirty minutes. Brother Schambach couldn't preach! He shut the book. He couldn't even pray! He asked everybody in the church to stand.

People had often asked my father, "Do I need the Holy Ghost?" When we encounter needs like this woman presented, a person doesn't have any idea how to pray. This is why we all need the fullness of the Holy Spirit!

The Holy Ghost began to pray through my father. He said it felt like somebody put a robe on him—it was the robe of the anointing for miracles, and he could feel the anointing. A double portion rested upon him as he prayed in tongues. Then, as he put it, he started to eavesdrop on the Holy Spirit by praying in English. When he began to pray in English, what he was saying shocked him:

"Lord, in the name of Jesus, convict the real killer through the Holy Ghost. Make him confess to the crime."

Inside, my father was kicking himself. He thought, *Shut up, dummy. The man has already been convicted.* He was asking God to get hold of the real killer. He didn't know, but the Holy Spirit knew this woman's son hadn't committed the crime. The Holy

Spirit was praying through my father saying, "Get hold of the real killer and make him confess."

After Dad finished praying, he looked at the woman and said, "Go home, go to bed—and sleep! Your son will not die in the electric chair!" Again he chastised himself, thinking, *Shut up, you dumb preacher! Remember, you have to come back here tomorrow night and preach!*

Sometimes the Holy Spirit will say things that are difficult for you to believe. Sometimes when you are preaching, you say things that startle you. But it isn't you talking, it is the Holy Spirit.

Are you ready for the outcome of this story?

Dad returned to his hotel and went to bed. He got up the next morning and went to the diner a block away. On his way in, he bought the *New York Daily News*. Glory! Did you ever shout looking at a newspaper? Well, he did. You know what the headlines said? *"Man's Life Spared from Electric Chair—Story on page 3."* He didn't eat breakfast. Oh, no. He sat down on that curb and tore open the paper to page three. Dad remembered what that newspaper said verbatim. He could tell you the name of the district attorney. His name was Mr. Hogan. The story read, "Last night at 9:40, Mr. Hogan received a phone call from a man." (Remember, it was 9:30 when the woman disturbed the service. At 9:40, God answered the woman's prayer. Oh, hallelujah!) The man on the other end said, "You are burning the wrong man."

"What do you mean? Who is this?" asked Mr. Hogan.

"Never mind who it is. But you have a man scheduled to die in the electric chair for the murder of a man in the upper Bronx. You found his body in a second-floor apartment, face down with stab wounds."

Mr. Hogan said, "How do you know this?"

He said, "I'm the one who committed the crime."

"Where are you?" Mr. Hogan asked.

He answered, "I am two blocks from a certain precinct. And I am on my way in to give myself up."

Mr. Hogan stopped the execution. He went to the precinct and interrogated the new suspect until three o'clock in the morning, going over the same question. "Why did you give yourself up?"

Repeatedly the same answer came, "Man, I never had any intentions of giving myself up. But when I called you last night, something got a hold of me and made me confess."

CHAPTER 1

THE KEYS TO
PARTNERING WITH GOD

Donna Schambach

Miracle stories are so powerful—how they build the faith of the believer! They leave each of us wanting more of God's power and more of God's partnership in our lives.

Many people who don't know God also have a keen interest in spiritual things. They sense there is something beyond themselves and understand there are some occurrences in life neither science nor the rational mind can explain.

The Bible introduces us to the world of the supernatural, and also gives us principles or keys to living in supernatural relationship with a living God. We need to understand these vital keys before we can live full lives with the Lord, and tap into His supernatural power to receive the anointing for miracles:

Key 1: Faith

Key 2: Holy Spirit Empowerment

Key 3: Compassion

Key 4: Authority

Key 5: Obedience

Key 6: Coveting

Key 7: Spiritual Perception

Key 8: Consecration and Holiness

When we study the Bible and come to understand the person of Jesus Christ, we recognize that Jesus is the central figure in all of the biblical accounts, revealing Father God's immense love for humankind and intense compassion toward each individual. Jesus also explained how all of the prophetic writings of the Old Testament pointed to Him and the plan of salvation He offered.

It is important to know that while Jesus is 100 percent God, having divine blood running through His veins, He was also 100 percent human, a new Adam, as the apostle Paul called Him, living out life on the earth in complete fellowship with and in obedience to the Father.

> *Consequently, just as one trespass resulted in condemnation for all people, so also one righteous act resulted in justification and life for all people.* **For just as through the disobedience of the one man [Adam] the many were made sinners, so also through the obedience of the one man [Jesus] the many will be made righteous** (Romans 5:18-19 NIV).

The Bible teaches that Jesus lived in sinless perfection. Yet, He did not use His divine attributes to live a godly life on earth; He lived in perfect unison with the Father by the *power of the Holy Spirit*. Jesus demonstrated through His own life how we were to live and minister once He left this earth.

We might say Jesus was spiritually "in-tune" to the frequency of Heaven's throne room, 24/7. He instinctively knew when and where to move and when to sit still. Jesus certainly knew when and what to speak, and always understood exactly what to do.

He spoke with an authority no one had ever heard and loved with a compassion that had never been expressed. Jesus had an unusual relationship with God, calling Him Father, and He never lost His childlike belief in the power of Abba's words. As a result, He operated in unusual spiritual gifts—prophesying, revealing, healing, and performing outstanding miracles everywhere He went.

This God-Man, with such unusual events surrounding His life, told His disciples something amazing:

> *I tell you the truth,* ***anyone who believes in me*** *will do* ***the same works*** *I have done, and* ***even greater works,*** *because I am going to be with the Father* (John 14:12 NLT).

This word, along with other things Jesus told them, began to open the door of possibilities to those closest to Him—but it would be much later until their eyes would open and they would understand the truth and weightiness of His words.

In the meantime, they would learn by His example. The way He lived His life in communion and fellowship with His heavenly Father was key to His earthly ministry.

CHAPTER 2

KEY #1: FAITH

Donna Schambach

In personality and demeanor my parents were polar opposites. Dad was loud and boisterous, drawing his strength from interacting with people. Mother, on the other hand, was quiet and reserved, content with retiring to the background.

If there was one trait they equally exhibited, though, it was childlikeness, particularly when it came to the things of the Spirit of God. They were transparent, humble folks who delighted in the Bible's truth and heartily believed everything Jesus ever spoke.

Dad became excited just *thinking* about miracles. When the power of God was at work in a service, he could stay and watch God work all night. It didn't matter if it was his meeting or someone else's—if God was moving, He wanted to behold the spectacle. His childlike fascination with the handiwork of God never diminished.

Mother had a love for heavenly things—she couldn't get enough of stories from people who had visited Heaven. She loved to hear about the ministry of angels and the moving of the Holy Spirit in revival moments. Often she rehearsed with wistful eyes amazing encounters she personally had in times of great revival outpourings. Those moments never left her spirit.

My parents lived young in Jesus, and I often heard people tell them how young they looked, even when they were well into their eighties. Their childlike wonder kept Jesus and the Word of God real in our household. I was truly privileged to grow up in a household and an atmosphere of childlike faith.

Trusting God was contagious in my home, especially when I was a child. My spiritual eyes were opened at a very young age. I had not yet learned to question my faith or allow doubt to overtake my thinking.

As though it were yesterday, I remember a specific time when I was 4 years of age. I was highly allergic to poison ivy and my wanderings in the woods one day left me exposed to the evil plant. All over my body, on every limb and crevice, was the bright red, itchy rash.

My parents were leaving for a ministry engagement for a few days, and Mother gave my grandmother one final instruction: "Mom, don't forget to put the calamine lotion on Donna before she goes to bed!" As my grandmother grunted out a very low and quiet "Mmm-hmm," we headed to our front steps to wave goodbye to my parents.

When their car passed out of sight, my grandmother took one long look at me and said, "Donna, do you believe Jesus can heal you of that poison ivy?"

I was 4, so I didn't philosophize nor debate theology. I only knew what I knew. My answer was an emphatic, carefree, "Yeah."

Mom-Mom sprang to her feet and hurried to get her trusty oil bottle. She anointed my head and prayed a simple prayer of healing. Then she instructed me to thank Jesus for healing my body. That was it.

She bathed me; put me to bed; and, oh yeah, she "forgot" to put the calamine lotion on that night.

When I awoke the next day, I realized I had spent the entire night asleep, without itching. Examining my arms and legs, it seemed I had brand-new skin with absolutely no signs of poison ivy. I was completely healed! As a 4-year-old I was "wowed" by God's power and so grateful to Jesus for healing me.

CHILDLIKE FAITH

I am a living testimony—childlike faith works.

As I grew older, though, I had enough naysayers and doubters in my high school and college years to influence the way I thought. As they asked their questions, it caused me to wonder why healing worked for some and not for others. I heard many discussions about "God's will," "God's sovereignty," and "living in a fallen world." They were all offered as possibilities as to why some never received miracles after seemingly having "all the faith in the world."

It's not my part to question one's faith, but I do know what Jesus said:

> *Then Jesus called a little child to Him, set him in the midst of them, and said, "Assuredly, I say to you, unless you are converted **and become as little children,** you will by no means enter the kingdom of heaven. Therefore **whoever humbles himself as this little child** is the greatest in the kingdom of heaven"* (Matthew 18:2-4).

Of course Jesus was referring to the humility of a child's heart to receive salvation and enter Heaven. Yet, the same humility that opens one's heart to the truth of salvation also opens the door to seeing everything Heaven has to offer. Continuing to walk in childlike humility and wonder is key to seeing miracles in our lives.

God has allowed me to glimpse the kingdom of Heaven at work many times, and the entrance was always the exercise of childlike faith and humility.

For example, one day we were traveling on Aeroflot, on our way from Petrapavlosk, Kamchakta, to Moscow—about a 9-hour flight. We had been on a historic, three-week mission, and we were ready to return home. This was the first leg of that homeward journey.

My dad was sitting in first class; I was by a window near the center of the plane; and our interpreter, Nikolai, from the Ukraine, was riding in the jump seat in the very back of the plane near the flight attendants.

About halfway through the flight I heard an announcement from the pilot. Since I did not understand Russian, the words had no effect on me…that is until Nikki showed up.

"Praise God, Sister Donna! Slava bo-hu!"

"Praise God, Nikki! How are you?"

"I am wonderful, Sister Donna. I have been witnessing to the flight attendants about Jesus and they do not want to hear anything. They are atheists. Just now the pilot made very important announcement. He said we are over Siberia and we are running out of fuel. We have very strong head wind and we must make emergency landing in Siberia."

My heart began to sink and race at the same time.

"Praise God!" Nikki continued, "I told them we have an American preacher on board whom God uses for many miracles. They asked me to find him and pray about this. They told me if God gets us out of this emergency, they would believe Jesus is alive. They are very afraid."

"Praise God, Nikki," I gulped. But I wasn't feeling it like Nikki was. He bounced to the front of the plane to find Dad, and I started to pray in tongues.

About two and a half hours later, I heard the same pilot over the intercom. Of course, I didn't understand his Russian any better the second time; but, it wasn't long before Nikolai came running to tell me what happened.

"Praise the Lord, Sister Donna!"

"Praise the Lord, Nikki! What happened?"

"Oh, it is so good! I told Brother Schambach what the pilot said and I asked him to pray. This is what he prayed, 'Lord, turn that head wind into a tailwind!'" (It was a simple, childlike prayer.)

"Well, the pilot just told everyone that the headwind went away and an unusual tailwind took its place. We are now scheduled to land in Moscow one hour early! No Siberia! Hallelujah!"

"Oh, praise God, Nikki!"

"And when the flight attendants heard the pilot, they were so amazed! They knew God had answered prayer. They received Jesus as their Savior, and they want to come to church with me on Sunday!" (At this point we were both shouting!)

Oh what a lesson! Childlike Nikki believed in the prayer of the man of God; he believed that Jesus would manifest Himself to those flight attendants who needed Him. And childlike Brother

Schambach trusted in the keeping power of Jesus to perform a miracle if need be—and Jesus did it!

Something else loomed in my spirit. I also knew I had to walk in greater humility before God. I had to trust Him as a child trusts her papa. My faith was weaker than those two...there was definitely more growing in faith ahead for me.

GROWING IN FAITH

Not too long after that trip, the Spirit of God began to deal with me strongly about praying for the sick in my meetings. I had just started to work with my father after a twelve-year career in Christian education. I had done some pastoral work, but I had never preached under a tent in the barrios of our nation—until I began working with Dad.

Up until that time I considered myself to be a good teacher and an adequate preacher. I could make a great outline for lessons or sermons; I knew how to add illustrations and life applications.

At that time, overhead projectors were popular, and I knew how to use one very well as a teaching aid. But when I began to preach to hundreds of people who lived, worked, and often struggled in the inner cities of our nation, I soon found out they didn't need a tailored sermon or an overhead projector.

The hurting people I faced did need the skillful preaching of God's Word to encourage their faith—but they needed more. Desperate people need *the anointing* of the Holy Spirit.

God wanted to set them free from drugs, alcohol, perversion, and all kinds of oppression. The Lord desired to heal their broken bodies and encourage their faith. We were sent into those city-centers to raise up believers to be strong in faith, trusting God for their households and their entire families—even their communities—to come to know Jesus!

One powerful afternoon in Baltimore, Maryland, I had just finished giving my altar call. People had responded with sincere hearts and tears, crying out to God for deliverance and transformation. I remember feeling a satisfaction in my soul because of that altar call and closing my Bible on the podium. As soon as it closed, I heard the voice of God in my spirit, "You're not done yet."

What do You mean, Lord? I wondered. Surely He felt as good about this altar call as I did. It seemed like a "wrap" to me.

"You haven't prayed for the sick yet," He said.

Now I was getting nervous. *Pray for the sick?* In my mind, that was not my thing. It was Dad's thing. He was the miracle worker in our family—and one was enough. Then my protests became more honest and God began to show me the core of the problem.

What if no one gets healed? screamed out of my head.

There it was: doubt, fear, and unbelief. God was about to teach me about putting childlike faith to work. Childlike faith is not a fruit of the flesh, but of the Spirit of God.

In my spirit I could hear the Holy Spirit coaching me, "Just do what I tell you to do."

I looked up and saw a lady to my right on the front row in a partial body cast. It extended from the top of her right hip all the way to her toes. As I interviewed her later, I learned a city bus hit her three years previously, and her leg never healed.

I knew God wanted me to pray for her, but secretly my heart was beating out of my chest. Couldn't God have pointed out someone with a headache or a bad chest cold?

Thankfully, the Lord was teaching me a lesson in childlike faith—when we humble ourselves, allow our fleshly concerns to die, and do what He tells us to do—amazing supernatural events begin to happen around us.

I am quite sure the Lord was chuckling a bit as I worked my way through this process. I was a novice in the working of miracles, figuring things out as I went.

I remember asking the woman in the hip cast why she came to the service that afternoon. Her response was an emphatic, "I came to be healed."

So, I folded her arm through mine, and asked her to do as I did.

"Let's take a walk!" I began. Then I delivered the most spiritual command I could think of, "Take the first step for the Father."

She obeyed me and put one foot on the ground. *So far so good*, I thought. "Now," I ventured, "Let's take a step for the Son."

(Oh, I sounded so religious—but remember, I was working my way through this miracle.)

Finally, I said, "Let's take a third step for the Holy…" Before I could say, "Holy Spirit," the woman let out a scream that would scare a banshee to death! She jumped up and down on both feet and ran around the tent as though she was shot out of a cannon!

The people attending the tent service were shouting and praising God, because they could see with their own eyes the woman was completely and entirely healed!

The faith preacher—you know the religious one taking religious steps of faith, me—was still standing in the front of the tent with my mouth wide open thinking, *Look at God!*

Oh, dear reader, I certainly cannot explain all of the ways we human beings tie in with the supernatural, healing power of God. He surprises me with new ways all the time. But this one thing I know, God loves it so much when His children trust Him. He loves it when we don't complicate things by overthinking them. He is so thrilled when we trust Him and accept His Word as truth with simple, childlike faith:

> *But without faith it is impossible to please Him, for he who comes to God must believe that He is, and that He is a rewarder of those who diligently seek Him* (Hebrews 11:6).

God wants to open some amazing doors into the supernatural realms for you. It is His good pleasure to give you the kingdom. The beginning place is humility, as a little child. As we humble ourselves and trust Daddy, our Father in Heaven, the kingdom's treasures are ours:

> *But Jesus called the children to him and said, "Let the little children come to me, and do not hinder them, for the kingdom of God belongs to such as these"* (Luke 18:16 NIV).

Why don't we pray about that together?

> *Father, I dare to call You Daddy. I thank You for inviting me to be part of Your own family, adopted as an heir to Your kingdom. Please forgive me for the times I have doubted You and Your Word. Forgive me for giving in to fear. Right now I humble myself before You.*
>
> *Would You do a new work in my heart? Would You restore to me the childlike spirit I had on the day of my salvation? Please let me hear Your voice more clearly than any other*

voice; and allow me to trust Your words more than any other words.

Give me a deeper dimension of childlike faith. I want to obey You so closely that daily I will follow You to people in need and minister Your love and healing power to them. Let this be a season of supernatural power for me. In Jesus' mighty name, amen.

Faith works in every dimension of our lives. I want you to read a few powerful faith-building miracle stories, told by my father, R. W. Schambach. Then, I will continue with the next key in operating with an anointing for miracles. That will be the pattern for this book. I will teach a little, and Dad will testify a little. I pray the Holy Spirit impresses a hunger for a richer anointing on your life greater than any you have experienced to date.

CHAPTER 3

FAITH-BUILDING MIRACLE STORIES

as told by R. W. Schambach

BROTHER LEROY GETS SAVED

In 1956 I was called back from the evangelistic field to bury my mama.

All of us remaining six kids were at her bedside when she died. She wasn't asking God to give her more life. My mother lived a full life. She had raised twelve kids. Six of us were left. Do you know what Mama was doing? She was crying out to God. She said, "Oh God, You promised me You would save all my children." Her dying cry was for her kids.

All of us were saved and filled with the Holy Ghost except my younger brother, Leroy. He was six feet four inches tall and 240 pounds of solid steel. He was standing next to me at our dying mother's bedside. I gave him a poke in the ribs—almost broke my elbow.

I said, "Come on, boy. Get right with God before Mom goes."

He said, "Hey, not now. Mama is dying." He loved Mom just as much as anybody, but he was a backslider.

We buried Mom. She died without seeing that answer. Does that mean God isn't faithful? Of course not. I went back to the evangelistic field. I was traveling with Brother Allen all the time. We were in California. I had a great burden for my brother. It hit me all of a sudden when Brother Allen was giving an altar call. I leaped off that platform. I jumped in the altar call for salvation.

Brother Allen said, "What are you doing there Schambach? The call is for sinners. It doesn't look good that my afternoon speaker is getting saved."

We are always making judgments on others, aren't we? We don't know what is going on in a person's heart. But I stayed there and said, "Lord, I am no longer R. W., I am Leroy. If he isn't going to get saved, I am going to get saved for him." Now, I had never heard anybody say that before, but I felt that. I wanted to get saved for him. I went into that prayer tent. I got on my face. I cried out to God.

The next day I had a call from my sister Margaret. I said, "Margaret, am I ever glad you called. I have some good news for you."

She said, "Will you let me talk? I am paying for this call."

I said, "You can talk when I get done. I have some good news. Leroy is saved!"

There was a silence on the phone.

I said, "Margaret, did you hear what I said?"

She said, "How did you know?"

I said, "How did I know? You don't know what I went through last night, girl." I told her how I took his place and answered the altar call, crying out to God to have mercy.

She said, "That's what I called to tell you. Last night we were all in church. All except Leroy. He was out living it up, having a ball. Halfway through the sermon, Leroy walked in. He didn't even stop to sit in a pew. He headed for the altar. He draped his six-feet-four frame over the altar and cried out to God. God saved him and filled him with the Holy Ghost."

Leroy didn't hear a sermon. Sometimes we preachers think we preach masterpieces. But people aren't getting saved because of the preaching. It is the Holy Ghost who takes them to the cross!

YOU DON'T HAVE ANY TROUBLE

There is a powerful confession that I have learned to hold on to in the midst of difficult circumstances. It is something that I have said to countless people throughout the years. I close my broadcasts by saying it. It has become my motto: You don't have any trouble… all you need is faith in God!

I learned that statement from a dear brother who had a personal encounter with the living Christ.

I was preaching in Buffalo, New York, when a gentleman invited me and my staff to his home for dinner. We enjoy invitations like that when we can because we get tired of quarter-pounders and French fries. One thing he forgot to tell me, however, is that he didn't live in Buffalo. He lived in Niagara Falls.

My meetings don't get out at nine o'clock. When you lay hands on thousands of people, it gets close to the midnight hour. After the meeting, we had to travel all the way to Niagara Falls. Whenever

I am invited out, I fast all day. I make sure I don't eat anything because I like to fill up while I am there.

The man's wife had outdone herself with the menu. It was one of the most bountiful tables I have ever seen. She had roast turkey, porterhouse steak, roast beef, and fried chicken. (In that part of the country, you don't invite a preacher unless you have fried chicken.) The gentleman asked me to pray. I blessed the food.

We were anxious to start eating, but when the man began to speak, what he had to say was more interesting than the food. I actually pushed my plate back to listen. He said he had never been sick a day in his life. He had money in the bank. His future was secure. He worked for the government. But all of a sudden something struck him—spinal meningitis—and paralyzed him from head to toe. He spent over three months in the hospital. Doctors were called in from all around the world. His bank account dwindled. He had to sell his home for the equity to pay the doctor bills. Rheumatoid arthritis crept into every joint until he couldn't stand the pain. He lapsed into a coma for almost four months.

Since the man was Roman Catholic, his priest was called to administer the last rites of that church. Lying in the coma, he knew what the priest was doing, but he couldn't communicate because he was paralyzed. "I couldn't flicker an eyelash," he recalled. How would you feel when you know that the priest is giving you the last rites—the last ceremony in the Catholic church before you die?"

As soon as the priest left, another priest walked through the wall and over to the bed. There was something different about this priest. He was dressed all in white. The new priest leaned down to the dying man and called him by name. He said, "You don't have any trouble. All you need is faith in God."

Of course, he was laying there thinking, *What kind of crazy priest is this? I don't have any trouble? Here I am in a coma. I can't communicate. There is arthritis in every joint. I have spinal meningitis. I had to sell my home. My bank account is gone. Is this not trouble?*

But the priest said, "I am Jesus of Nazareth, and I am going to heal you right now."

Isn't that beautiful? Jesus said, "When I walk out of this room, I want you to get out of this bed. Shave, wash, and walk out of this hospital. Go to the first bookstore you can find and buy a Bible. Start reading from Saint John's Gospel. You will find the way to eternal life."

Oh, hallelujah! The man told us that Jesus turned and walked right back through the wall. As the man was telling me this story, he looked at me and said, "Brother Schambach, I wonder why Jesus didn't just use the door."

I said, "He is the door!"

He can make an entrance wherever you are. He can come right into your automobile. He can visit you on your job. He can walk into your bedroom. No matter where you are, Jesus is the door. He will come in!

When Jesus walked out of that room, the man got out of bed and started shaving. The nurse came tip-toeing in. She wanted to pull the sheet over because the other priest had walked out. But she saw the bed empty. She ran into the bathroom and said, "Please get back into bed. Don't you know you're dying? The priest gave you the last rites."

The man said to her, "Cool it, honey. Another Priest came in and gave me the 'first rites' all over again. I'm going to live!"

OXYGEN TANK MIRACLE

A young 17-year-old girl in New York was dying with tuberculosis. One lung had collapsed. The other one was half gone. She was in an oxygen tank.

She attended a denominational church. The folks in her church loved God and were saved. However, they didn't believe in divine healing. Of course, divine healing doesn't make us Christians. The blood of Jesus makes us Christians because He paid the price for our salvation at Calvary.

This young girl was dying. Her physician, who was a Christian, told her, "You are going to die, and there is nothing we can do. Tuberculosis has set in. One lung is gone. The other is half gone. I am going to send you home so that you can spend your remaining days with your family."

She was breathing pure oxygen. She lay in an oxygen tent waiting for death. She was 17 years of age and had dwindled to 67 pounds. She was a lovely young lady, but she was wasting away. Don't you tell me God does that to people. I wouldn't serve a God who did that. God is a good God. He promises beauty for ashes.

> *The thief does not come except to steal, and to kill, and to destroy. I have come that they may have life, and that they may have it more abundantly* (John 10:10).

The doctor sent the girl home to die. She lay there with her head up so she could read her Bible. She resigned herself to the fact that she was going to die. This is what she had been taught. You are only what you are taught. That is why you have to be careful where you go to church. I can't say that strongly enough. The girl lay in that position, reading Peter's epistle, *"Who Himself bore our sins in His own body on the tree, that we, having died to sins, might live for righteousness...*" (1 Peter 2:24). When she read those words, she put her Bible down and began to praise God.

Weeping, she said, "Oh, Lord, I will be so glad to see You. I know I am going to die. Doctors can't do any more for me. But thank You for saving me. Thank You for washing me in the blood." She worshiped and thanked God for saving her and went back to reading the same verse she had just read in the Bible.

"Himself bore our sins in His own body on the tree, that we, having died to sins, might live for righteousness..." But she didn't stop there this time. She went right on in that same verse, "*...by whose stripes you were healed.*" The words lit up like a neon sign. She said, "Oh, look what I found." There was no preacher there to preach to her. No one was there but the Word.

She said, "Lord, I just finished praising You for the first part, now I am going to praise You for the second part. You have already healed me. Jesus, I'm sorry I won't be seeing You right now. I plan on staying around here awhile."

Isn't that beautiful faith? Hallelujah! "I won't be coming like I planned," she said. "I have changed my mind because I just found some truth—and truth is what sets us free." She started praising God for perfect health. She didn't gain weight instantly. She still weighed 67 pounds. But she unzipped that oxygen tent and hollered for her mother, "Mama, come quick!"

Her mother thought this was the day her daughter was going to die. She came stumbling up the stairs. "What is it, baby? What is it?"

"Oh, Mama, look what I found. Read this."

Her mother mumbled through the words, then said, "I read it. Lay down now."

The daughter said, "Oh, you didn't read it right. Won't you read it? Mama, it says I'm healed. Two thousand years ago Jesus healed me."

Isn't it strange how some people can read God's Word and get nothing out of it? The mother looked at her daughter and started crying.

"What's wrong, Mama? What are you crying about?"

"The doctor told me that on the day you were to die, you would lose your mind," the mother said.

Isn't it strange that when you want to trust God, people think you are losing your mind? When you are willing to die, you are normal. "It's all right to get religious, but you don't have to carry that too far. Don't be a fanatic!" You don't have to believe that.

Her mother tucked her back in. But the girl said, "Mama, I'm not going to die. Go downstairs and make me breakfast. I want some bacon and eggs, orange juice, whole wheat toast, and coffee."

Mama said, "Now I know you have lost your mind. You haven't eaten anything in ten months."

She said, "I haven't heard such powerful truth in ten months. Go down and make my breakfast. I'm getting out of here."

The girl's mother tucked her in and sneaked out of the room. No sooner had she closed the door than the girl unzipped the oxygen tent. She pulled her scrawny legs out of the bed and hobbled over to her dresser. She picked out one of the dresses that she had worn when she was 120 pounds. It looked like a robe on her now. She put slippers on her feet and started down the stairs. She went to the kitchen, opened the door and asked, "Are my bacon and eggs ready?" She sat down to have breakfast and said, "Lord, bless this food to my brand-new body. I am not going to die. I am going to live."

She went to her doctor the next day. The X-rays found two brand-new lungs and no sign of tuberculosis.

She went on to live in New York. She married and gave birth to four children. This was all possible because she heard the truth and dared to believe it.

CHAPTER 4

KEY #2: HOLY SPIRIT EMPOWERMENT

Donna Schambach

Before Jesus performed one miracle, He had an encounter in the Jordan River. A heavenly portal opened upon Him when John the Baptist was baptizing Him. His ceremonial baptism was not for remission of sins, but for initiation into the priesthood of Heaven.

When the heavens opened, the Father spoke and the Holy Spirit descended on Him in the form of a dove:

> *One day when the crowds were being baptized, Jesus himself was baptized. As he was praying, the heavens opened, and the Holy Spirit, in bodily form, descended on him like a dove. And a voice from heaven said, "You are my dearly loved Son, and you bring me great joy." Jesus was about thirty years old when he began his public ministry..."* (Luke 3:21-23 NLT).

All other monumental events in Jesus' life took place after this one extraordinary day. His major confrontation with satan; His ordination day in Nazareth; the miracle at the wedding of Cana; the feeding of the 5,000—all of the miracles—every work of the Holy Spirit through Jesus happened after He was baptized in water and by the Holy Spirit.

As a pattern, this order is very important. Before we seek to operate in the gifts of the Spirit, it is vitally important to seek the empowerment of the Spirit. This empowering experience, usually coming at the same time or after our salvation experience, is a release of the Holy Spirit's power—the power of the One who already lives inside every believer.

The first work of the Spirit Jesus mentioned was a bubbling spring—springing up and watering the individual who received the salvation the Spirit offered. When the Holy Spirit entered, He would teach each believer how to worship God "in spirit and in truth."

Jesus talked to the Samaritan woman at the well, explaining the life-giving power of the Holy Spirit, comparing Him to a refreshing spring of water:

> *Jesus replied, "Anyone who drinks this water will soon become thirsty again. But **those who drink the water I give** will never be thirsty again. It becomes a fresh, bubbling spring within them, **giving them eternal life**"* (John 4:13-14 NLT).

Here Jesus was referencing the work of salvation by the Holy Spirit when He comes to live in a believer's heart.

Jesus also talked about water that "will flow *from* his heart." This work of the Holy Spirit imparts life to those around the believer, releasing power for salvation, healing, deliverance, and life to anyone who has a need!

It happened in Jerusalem where Jesus was observing the Feast of Tabernacles. Perhaps He was watching the procession of the proud priests who carried pitchers of water on their heads as they proceeded from the temple. They were visually and symbolically reminding God's people of the life of the Spirit of God flowing from His temple.

Jesus also knew the traditions were often lost on both priests and average citizens. They had feasts, traditions, sound theology, and dead religion; they needed real, spiritual life—new, fresh, divine life and the power for change in all of their trials.

I picture Jesus laying low watching the ceremonies for several days, but on the last day of the feast—the day of the water ceremony—He could hold it in no longer. He wanted God's people to know the Father had so much more to offer them:

> *On the last day, the climax of the festival, Jesus stood and shouted to the crowds, "Anyone who is thirsty may come to me! Anyone who believes in me may come and drink! For the Scriptures declare, 'Rivers of living water will flow from his heart.'"* (When he said "living water," he was speaking of the Spirit, who would be given to everyone believing in him. But the Spirit had not yet been given, because Jesus had not yet entered into his glory.) (John 7:37-39 NLT).

A beautiful word picture of this work is found in Ezekiel 47:

> *There will be swarms of living things wherever the water of this river flows. Fish will abound in the Dead Sea, for its waters will become fresh.* **Life will flourish wherever**

this water flows. Fishermen will stand along the shores of the Dead Sea. All the way from En-gedi to En-eglaim, the shores will be covered with nets drying in the sun. Fish of every kind will fill the Dead Sea, just as they fill the Mediterranean. ...Fruit trees of all kinds will grow along both sides of the river. The leaves of these trees will never turn brown and fall, **and there will always be fruit on their branches.** *There will be a new crop every month, for they are watered by the river flowing from the Temple.* **The fruit will be for food and the leaves for healing** (Ezekiel 47:9-12 NLT).

What a picture of the life-giving stream flowing and bringing life to everything it touched! This happened in the life of Jesus after He was baptized in the Holy Spirit, and it happened in every one of the disciples when they obeyed the first command He gave them after His resurrection:

And now I will send the Holy Spirit, just as my Father promised. But stay here in the city until the Holy Spirit comes and fills you with power from heaven (Luke 24:49 NLT).

This command was repeated in Acts 1:

...Do not leave Jerusalem until the Father sends you the gift he promised, as I told you before. John baptized with water, but in just a few days you will be baptized with the Holy Spirit. ...But you will receive power when the Holy Spirit comes upon you. And you will be my witnesses, telling people about me everywhere—in Jerusalem, throughout Judea, in Samaria, and to the ends of the earth (Acts 1:4,8 NLT).

The disciples obeyed Jesus, and on the Day of Pentecost, 120 people met for prayer in an upper room of a house in Jerusalem. The initial baptism of the Holy Spirit had unique characteristics, including a rushing, mighty wind blowing through the upper room and tongues of fire sitting upon each believer's head.

Yet one expression of the Holy Spirit's baptism remaining throughout the Book of Acts when the disciples prayed for believers to receive "the gift" of the Holy Spirit, was speaking in other tongues.

This Holy Spirit phenomenon exists today in multitudes empowered by the Holy Spirit. Many believe this expression is the constant because the Holy Spirit wants to claim our tongues for His purposes. Rather than allowing our tongues to speak doubt, unbelief, lies, negativity, cursing, or coarse jesting, we yield control to the Holy Spirit, as He fills our hearts and mouths with praises and blessings and wonderful words of power and encouragement.

Just as in the life of Jesus, it was also true for the disciples who were baptized in the Holy Spirit. Immediately they changed from being followers to leaders. They went from being questioners to powerful preachers and proclaimers of the Word. The disciples became apostles—sent to wreak havoc on the enemy's territory with signs, wonders, and miracles.

Often I heard Papa say the Acts of the Apostles should really be called the Acts of the Holy Spirit. A new era of salvation and grace entered on the Day of Pentecost, and the Holy Spirit birthed the Church of Jesus Christ all around the world. Today, He is still at work convincing hearts that Jesus is alive and doing the things He did 2,000-plus years ago.

Dear reader, if you want to have an increased sensitivity to the moving of the Holy Spirit, hearing His voice, and seeing with His eyes, you may first need to ask Jesus to baptize you in the Holy Spirit with the expression of speaking in tongues. Ask the Holy Spirit to empower you and take over your thought and speech patterns. Let Him know you want to be entirely consecrated to His work here on earth, demonstrating the Gospel of Good News.

Your prayer doesn't have to be anything sophisticated or fancy. You can pray something simple with me, right now:

Father, in the name of Jesus the Great Baptizer, I thank You that You give every good and perfect gift. You said if Your children ask for the Holy Spirit, You would give Him to us. I know the Holy Spirit already lives in my heart, but I also want to be overwhelmed by His presence and power. I want to speak in tongues; I want to heal the sick; I want my words to be prophetic and encouraging; I want everything You have to give me. And so, I praise You and worship You now and thank You for hearing and answering prayer!

That's right. As you pray, feel the presence of the Holy Spirit cover you like a warm blanket. You may feel a volcanic rumbling in your stomach area—that is where your "heart" or "spirit self" communicates. Just release the flow through your mouth and the Holy Spirit will give you something to say—He will begin to worship God through you in another language! Oh, hallelujah, may 1,000 tongues of every nation and people group praise the mighty name of Jesus!

The language the Holy Spirit gives you may remain the same for a while, but the more you pray in the Spirit, you may pray in new languages, some you recognize and some you don't. My father said when he was baptized in the Holy Spirit, two friends of his told him they heard him preaching and praising God fluently in their native languages: Italian and Greek. When I was baptized in the Spirit, my new languages were Spanish and French.

Since that time God has given me many different languages and dialects. I have detected African languages, Asian, and Native American. Then sometimes I just burst forth into singing in heavenly languages, tongues that are not recognized here on earth.

Praying in the Holy Spirit is a wonderful adventure and also a powerful spiritual strengthening and encouragement: *"But you, beloved, building yourselves up on your most holy faith, praying in the Holy Spirit"* (Jude 1:20).

When we don't know how or what to pray, the apostle Paul tells us the Holy Spirit is the answer:

> *Likewise the Spirit also helps in our weaknesses. For we do not know what we should pray for as we ought, but the Spirit Himself makes intercession for us with groanings which cannot be uttered. Now He who searches the hearts knows what the mind of the Spirit is, because He makes intercession for the saints according to the will of God* (Romans 8:26-27).

When we pray in the Holy Spirit, we keep our hearts and minds in tune with the voice, the eye, and the will of God. It is our way of keeping a clear channel to the things of the supernatural.

Perhaps that is why the apostle Paul wrote, *"I thank my God I speak with tongues more than you all"* (1 Corinthians 14:18). He certainly had a lot of obstacles to confront in his monumental mission—he had to stay in communication with God at all times.

Do not be discouraged if the first time you pray for the baptism of the Holy Spirit you don't experience speaking in tongues. Sometimes that manifestation comes when we are not concentrating so hard on receiving it. Oftentimes it comes when we are lost in worship, sensing the presence of God, being filled up with Him! Don't worry! He wants to baptize you fully—it is His free gift to you.

***

My father was such a great storyteller—he absolutely loved to tell miracle stories—especially ones he witnessed with his own eyes and in his own ministry. I am sure you will enjoy the three in the next chapter that emphasize what it is like to minister in the leading and the power of the Holy Spirit.

CHAPTER 5

HOLY GHOST MIRACLE STORIES

*as told by **R. W. Schambach***

PRIZEFIGHTER GOES DOWN FOR THE COUNT

When I was pastoring in Newark, New Jersey, there was a dear woman in our church named Sister Price. She came to me one night about her husband. He was an old "boozer." All he did was drink. No matter how hard she tried, she could never get him to come to church with her.

She said, "Brother Schambach, you don't know what kind of devil I married. I've done everything for him, but he won't come to church with me. I've tried everything. I'm tired of it!"

"Well, I'm glad you're tired of it," I told her.

"You mean I can leave him?"

"Oh no, girl," I said. "You picked him out all by yourself. You said you're tired of it? Good. Now we're going to put it in God's hands."

So I laid hands on her and said, "Holy Ghost, sic him! Knock him down and drag him to the foot of the cross!"

I was running a revival there in Newark, so we had a service the next night. During the meeting, this big guy came in. He was about six-feet-two, 270 pounds. Solid steel! And he came walking up the center aisle like he owned the place.

I jumped off the platform and headed down toward him. I was walking like I owned the place. I met him face to face, head-on, jaw to jaw—an irresistible force meeting an immovable object.

"Are you the preacher?"

"Yes, sir," I said. "I'm the man of God here."

"They tell me you can help me."

"You smell like you need help, brother."

Then he said sarcastically, "You want to help me? Buy me a fifth of liquor!"

I felt my fist doubling up. The old Schambach was coming alive, the one who's supposed to be crucified with Christ. Do you know what I'm talking about? I wanted to give him a knuckle sandwich right there! But my hand went limp. The Holy Ghost wouldn't allow me to hit him. And boy, am I glad! I found out later that he was an all-state boxing champ!

So I went to lay hands on him, but the Holy Ghost wouldn't even let me touch him. I got about two inches from him and he just fell back—*bam!* He hit solid concrete!

Then Sister Price ran out shouting, "Aaahh! Glory! That's that devil I'm married to!"

I said, "Hush, woman. Don't say any more. He's here now. Let the Holy Ghost do His job now." So he lay there on the floor.

When he got up, he was sober and ready to receive Christ as his Savior. God saved him and filled him with the Holy Ghost and fire. He was speaking in other tongues and praising God!

God worked a miracle! He made a lamb out of a lion. After that, Brother Price preached the Gospel for many years in New York, New Jersey, Virginia, North Carolina, and all over the East Coast. He went on home to be with the Lord, but his wife, dear Sister Georgia Price, continued singing and telling the story of how God made her violent old husband a new creature through the delivering power of Jesus Christ.

FROM JUNK TO JESUS

I have many friends who have helped partner with my ministry over the years. A lot of them have great stories of what God has done for them through my ministry. I'll never forget the story of a certain partner of mine, Brother James Wallace, another "lost cause" who was transformed by the power of Christ.

In August 1975 I had my tent up in the Bronx, New York. Many preachers are afraid to go into the ghetto—into places like the Bronx. But I love to take the Gospel where it is needed! I love to take it right into the heart of the inner city. To see God perform miracles and deliver those who are bound by the devil. You see, a lot of these folks won't set foot in a church. So I bring church to them. People who wouldn't go into a church come pouring into my tent meetings, and that's when God takes over!

Now, James Wallace was just that kind of person. He was raised in one of the most hellish neighborhoods of the Bronx. At an early age he had experimented with many different types of pills and drugs, and as a teenager he became an alcoholic.

Circumstances from his environment and his own young rebellion filled him with a violent rage. He broke the law often and found himself in and out of police precincts and jail. James adopted the attitudes of his environment—he trusted no one but himself. Eventually he became a racist, hating all white people.

In his early twenties, James was living with his girlfriend, not wanting to marry her because he knew he would be a high-risk father in many ways. Life went from bad to worse when the doctors told him he had cirrhosis of the liver. James needed help.

In the eyes of man, he was not a likely candidate for salvation. But what is impossible with man is possible with God!

One day James pulled up in his car to 149th Street and the Major Deegan Expressway in the Bronx. He was parked in front of a Gospel tent that was as big as a football field. It looked like a circus tent. All he could hear was the voice of a preacher who was shouting about something.

James felt anger rising up within him. The preacher was a white man, and as far as he could tell, he was preaching about a white God named Jesus. Against his better judgment, James went inside to see what was happening.

That preacher was me, and I was telling people that Jesus could free them from sin, heal their bodies, and deliver them from addictions.

Then, I asked some people from the vast audience to come forward and tell others what Jesus had done for them. James heard stories of deaf ears opening, drug addicts being instantly set free, and people being healed from cancer. One thread of every story was the same—each of the storytellers said Jesus had done the work in their lives.

At first, James refused to believe what he was hearing. He thought all preachers were either pimps or sissies. Yet, James could not deny there was something powerful and real happening under that tent.

Night after night he would come back to listen. Then one night James mustered up the courage to go forward and let the preacher pray for him.

When I prayed for him, James said a prayer, "God, if You're real, let me feel something."

James didn't feel anything right away. In his mind he was saying, "See, I knew this thing was fake. Nothing happened."

He went right across the street to the bar and ordered some drinks.

But that night he realized something. He had lost his taste and needs for alcohol. He had no more shakes. He had no withdrawal symptoms. He was free from alcohol, and he knew it.

The next night, James went back to the tent. He knelt at an altar and asked Jesus Christ to forgive him. When James got off his knees, he was delivered from his addictions and healed of cirrhosis of the liver. Today, he is married, has four children, and is pastoring a church in the Bronx.

James is still partnering with my ministry today. He serves as a testimony of the power of God to set the captives free! In his own words:

"Jesus is the answer. He has set me free from pushing dope to preaching hope. From crime to Christ. From junk to Jesus."

IT'S NEVER TOO LATE

Some time ago, when I was in Seattle, Washington, I preached a message about Lazarus. The Bible says that Lazarus had been in the grave four days when Jesus finally came. Although it seemed as if He had arrived too late, He was right on time. He is never too late. In other words, it's never too late for a miracle.

Sometimes we put time limits on God. Mary and Martha were limited in their faith. They said to Jesus, *"Lord, if You had been here, my brother would not have died"* (John 11:21,32). They had forgotten that Jesus was Christ, the Son of God—Emmanuel: God with us. They had forgotten that Jesus is the Resurrection and the Life.

They didn't know that Jesus had intentionally waited. He wanted His followers to witness His miraculous power.

We should never try to figure out God's timetables. He is always on time. It's never too late.

After the service, a woman came to me and shoved a piece of paper into my hand. She said, "Now, I dare you to say it's not too late." Do you know what the paper was? A divorce paper, a final decree. She had just received it from the judge. It was final. The husband was gone. She looked me right in the eye and said again, "Now, I dare you to say it's not too late."

So I smiled and took her dare and said, "It's not too late."

She said, "What about that paper?"

I said, "You are looking at the wrong paper. My paper says, *'Therefore what God has joined together, let not man separate'* (Matthew 19:6). That is what I believe. How long have you been married?" She told me they had been married for twenty-seven years and had five children. I said, "That man has no business leaving you." I laid hands on her and said, "Holy Ghost, bring that rascal to his senses and save him. Don't bring him back home the way he is. Lord, save him and fill him with the Holy Ghost." I looked at the woman and said, "Go home and get ready for your husband. He is coming."

Of course, that was easy for me to say. I was leaving town. I am an evangelist. I can hit them and run. But in all honesty, I believed what I had said. My wife and I drove from Seattle to Philadelphia. When we got to Philly, I had a letter, from that woman, waiting for me. I opened it, and the first lines said, "Dear Brother Schambach, God is never too late! God got a hold of that rascal, saved him, and filled him with the Holy Ghost. The Lord brought him back home, and we got married all over again."

That is the powerful aspect of faith. Take a stand of faith and say, "Devil, you are a liar. I am going to believe God for a miracle because He is going to turn this situation around." Speak faith. Speak to that mountain, and that mountain has to obey your words. That is how you will experience the power of faith.

CHAPTER 6

KEY #3: COMPASSION

Donna Schambach

It was a Friday night youth service, early in Dad's pastoring days in Western Pennsylvania. The entire church had been passionately pursuing God's presence with prayer and fasting for about a week. Sharon, one of the young ladies in the church who had received a mighty miracle in her eye as a child, was now stretching her faith for her backslidden brother to surrender to the Lord Jesus as Savior.

Sharon called "Brother Schambach" to help her intercede for her brother's salvation. As a young pastor, Dad decided to fast seven days for the young man, believing God for his total deliverance.

Everyone was excited the Friday night of that week when Sharon's brother arrived sporting a black leather jacket with the symbol of a local biker club. He sat in one of the pews in the back, leaning against the wall. (Dad always said he had those pews built against the wall, so, if necessary, he could keep any of his targets from escaping while he preached to them.)

When young Pastor Schambach spotted the youth, God's compassion began reaching out to the young man, who was trying to hide on the back pew. Walking to the very pew where he was sitting, Brother Schambach body-blocked the exit and addressed the teenage biker:

"Young man, you don't know me, but I turned down twenty-one meals for you this week. Your sister told me you have been running from God, and I've come to tell you this is your night to stop running. God loves you and He is calling you. Tonight is your night!"

Even with all of Dad's pleadings, the young biker was like a slippery fish jumping out of the net. He brushed past the man of God anxiously resisting, "Not tonight, Preach! I'm too young!"

Dad told me he felt defeated that night. He knew the compassion of Jesus was reaching out to the young man—compassion for both him and Sharon who loved her wayward brother so deeply.

At 3 o'clock the next morning, Dad was awakened by another phone call from Sharon. As soon as he heard her voice, and the sobbing with which she talked, his heart sank. "Brother Schambach, will you preach my brother's funeral?"

"Oh no, Sharon!" he gasped, "What happened?"

"When my brother left the church, his eyes must have been wet with tears. The temperature was sub-zero, and when he put his helmet on, it must have fogged up the visor. Police said my brother lost control of his bike and it jumped over the median. As it did, it came face to face with an 18-wheeler climbing the hill, and my brother was buried into the grill of that truck. Brother Schambach, my brother was only 17 years old!"

Dad recalled often, he didn't sleep that night. He could only think about how close Sharon's brother was to eternity—how close he was to receiving Jesus. Underscored in his thinking was the brevity of every life—and how important the moment to receive Christ is. Truly, when a person is confronted with an opportunity to receive Jesus as Savior, it is a sacred, weighty moment.

As Brother Schambach arrived at the funeral parlor, on the street were about 150 black-jacketed motorcycle club members, smoking weed and cussing. The preacher walked through their "fog" and asked, "Are you going to pay respects to your buddy inside? You're either gonna get it from me inside, or out here on the curb."

All 150 filed into the funeral home. Dad grabbed the casket and wheeled it right in front of the entire motorcycle club. Pointing to it, he declared, "Here lie the remains of your buddy. His soul is in hell tonight."

Gasps went up all over the room, but Brother Schambach didn't back down. He told the story of the last week of their buddy's life—about his sister's agonizing and his pastor's prayer and fasting. In detail Dad described the invitation he gave to their buddy and his refusal to accept Christ. He spoke of the young man's desire to enjoy his youth and his total ignorance of being moments away from eternity.

At that precise moment, when it seemed as though all was lost, the compassion of the Father was still reaching out, this time to 150 teenagers who needed a Savior.

The power of the Father's compassion must have been strong in that room, because there, beside the coffin, all 150 club members knelt, crying out to God for forgiveness and asking Jesus into their hearts.

It was a powerful miracle, birthed out of prayer, fasting, and most of all, the compassionate heart of God.

My father and I often discussed that story because he told it many, many times, just as he was giving an altar call. (That story encouraged multiplied thousands to receive Jesus as Savior.)

The part of the story that revealed his tears, spoke to me of a softening heart. I mentioned to Dad that perhaps the young man was talking to the Father as he left the church that night—perhaps he took advantage of those moments and cried out for forgiveness.

Dad agreed, the compassionate heart of God keeps working with a person, until the very last minute—until it is too late.

WHY WAIT?

I have more to share about God's compassion in just a moment, but I believe you may be one with whom God's compassion is dealing right now. You may have wondered if God exists. Perhaps, should God really exist, you've wondered if He cares about you personally.

God uses so many ways to speak to people. Sometimes He uses a preacher, a neighbor, or a friend to share the love of Jesus. And sometimes He uses a book just like this one.

If you know you are not in right standing with God, why wait another minute? Right now you can receive His overture of love and compassion. He wants to come into your heart, cleanse you from every sin, and help you solve every problem in your life. He will set you free from fear, anxiety, addictions—He wants to take full control of your life.

You don't have to change one thing. All you have to do is humble yourself and repent of your sins. Surrender your life to Him. Jesus will become your personal Friend, and the Holy Spirit will become your Teacher, showing you how to live a life pleasing to the Father.

If we confess our sins, He is faithful and just to forgive us our sins and to cleanse us from all unrighteousness (1 John 1:9).

if you confess with your mouth the Lord Jesus and believe in your heart that God has raised Him from the dead, you will be saved (Romans 10:9).

Why don't you pray with me now?

Father, in the mighty name of Jesus, I humble myself before You today. I recognize I am in need of a Savior. I ask You to forgive me of all of my sins. I accept the work of Jesus on the cross as the sacrifice He made for my sins. Please come live in my heart and show me how to live for You. Right now, I thank You, that I am born again.

If you prayed that simple prayer from your heart, I believe you are already experiencing a feeling of cleansing and a release from the burden of sin. You can take a moment to thank Jesus for your precious new salvation experience.

Just as compassion reaches out to touch the hearts of men and women and beckons them to receive Jesus, His compassion also reaches out to heal sick bodies.

HOLY SPIRIT EMOTION

The Holy Spirit loves when His compassion flows from our hearts to help others. Anyone who wants to be used of God to see people healed and delivered will become very familiar with this "Holy Spirit emotion."

I had my first experience with this Spirit-emotion when I was 19 years of age. I was in college in Springfield, Missouri, and a group of my friends and I drove to Kansas City for the day—we had a day of shopping in mind.

At this time in my life I knew Jesus as my Savior and I was strong in the Holy Spirit, but I had no idea I would ever be called into public ministry. I was in college to study English and get a teaching degree—something I could "fall back on" until I was married one day. Public ministry was the farthest thing from my mind.

In the midst of shopping, I happened to walk into the public restroom of the huge Kansas City mall. There I saw an elderly woman standing at the sink trying to wash her hands. Her hands were trembling so badly she could hardly get soap out of the dispenser.

I went into the stall, and when I came out she was still at the sink. As I stood at the sink beside her I had the strongest, overwhelming urge to lay hands on her and command her to be healed in Jesus' name. In my heart I knew if I laid hands on her she would be healed.

For the first time in my life I was sensing the compassion of the Holy Spirit prompting me to do His work right there in the public restroom!

*But...*I didn't listen! I immediately panicked with fear; my mind raced with thoughts of rejection or being misunderstood; it was too public a place—I found a number of reasons *not* to do what the Holy Spirit had placed in my heart to do.

When I left the mall, I was so deeply convicted. I knew I had not only disobeyed the leading of the Holy Spirit, but I felt as though I had truly grieved Him.

A little time later, I was watching Johnny Carson's late night show because Billy Graham was going to be interviewed. I was intrigued when Johnny asked Dr. Graham if he ever had the desire to pray for sick people.

I was even more stunned when I heard Dr. Graham say something like, "Yes, I have felt the urging of the Holy Spirit to lay my hands on people from time to time. I remember in particular meeting a blind woman and I just knew if I laid hands on her in the name of Jesus, she would have been healed. But I never did it because of fear and embarrassment."

PROMPTING OF COMPASSION

My spirit stirred because I knew Billy Graham had felt the same prompting of compassion I had. And he confessed to the same response. His openness helped me to understand God is a loving, compassionate Father who wants to see many people healed and well. He is just looking for people with childlike faith and the will to obey Him when He nudges us.

The Spirit-emotion we call *compassion* is and always has been a catalyst for the supernatural power of God to be expressed in healing and miracles. We can see it at work in the ministry of Jesus:

Compassion fed 5,000 hungry people: *"Jesus called his disciples to him and said, 'I have compassion for these people, they have already been with me three days and have nothing to eat. I do not want to send them away hungry, or they may collapse on the way'"* (Matthew 15:32 NIV).

Compassion healed many who were sick: *"When Jesus went out He saw a great multitude; and He was moved with compassion for them, and healed their sick"* (Matthew 14:14).

Compassion performed outstanding miracles: *"So Jesus had compassion and touched their eyes. And immediately their eyes received sight, and they followed Him"* (Matthew 20:34).

Compassion raised the dead: *"When the Lord saw her, He had compassion on her and said to her, "Do not weep." Then He came and touched the open coffin, and those who carried him stood still. And He said, "Young man, I say to you, arise"* (Luke 7:13-14).

Compassion is often the motivator for a miracle. Many Christians pray for greater anointing, but if the Holy Spirit lives inside us, the anointing already resides within us.

Others pray for greater miracles—not a bad prayer. But how many pray for greater *compassion?* How many desire to hurt for people and feel their pains and anguish? How many desire to stand for hours to minister to those who are lost and hurting?

Compassion requires giving of one's self—offering up one's body as a living sacrifice—for the purpose of seeing the supernatural power of God released for healing, miracles, and raising the dead!

The Church is in dire need of the expressed gift of compassion; we all need a fresh dose of godly compassion operating through us.

My dad had compassion oozing out of his pores. He always took time for people. Many were the times I'd direct him off the platform because the length of the prayer lines was wearing him out physically.

I have seen God use Dad in extraordinary ways, through his heart of compassion. One long-time friend of mine, Elisabeth from Norway, was healed of Stage 4 lung cancer when Dad embraced her as a father hugging his daughter. This was the first time they met, but she felt a sensation like warm honey cover her—and she was healed that day.

Doctors had told Elisabeth and her husband, Alvaro, they would never have children because the chemo treatments had destroyed her reproductive organs. The doctors were wrong because they hadn't counted on the compassion of Jesus. Elisabeth was so very healed that God gave her two children, Samuel and Victoria, who are both serving God in ministry today!

What could God do if every one of His people would begin to yield to the promptings of the Holy Spirit and love people to their healing and deliverance?

CHRIST'S COMPASSION

I am very happy God has given me many more opportunities to yield to His compassionate promptings.

When I used to work in the Bronx, I was a regular at a local diner, and I had a favorite waitress. One day during the busiest part of the lunch shift, she told me she had been to doctor after doctor, including specialists, for her allergies, and she couldn't get rid of her cough and nasal congestion. It was affecting her sleep patterns and her ability to work. She was miserable.

Well, in the middle of my meal, I felt a holy prompting and I asked her to follow me to the back of the diner. I told her God wanted me to pray for her. So right there in the diner, in a room filled with strangers, we called on the name of Jesus for complete healing and deliverance from the allergies.

The very next time I entered the diner, she ran over to me, thanking me for the prayer. Her allergies were clearing up—and she was off all medication. She told me as we prayed she felt the presence of Jesus, and that moment changed the way she thought about God!

This is such an important lesson. Healing is one work of God's compassion that causes people to respond to His love:

Or do you despise the riches of His goodness, forbearance, and longsuffering, not knowing that the goodness of God leads you to repentance? (Romans 2:4)

Oh beloved reader, compassion is a powerful tool in God's hand!

During a very cold winter in Winnipeg, Manitoba, Canada, I was ministering in a prayer line with so many different kinds of pain manifesting in people's bodies. I sensed much of it was from demonic activity.

The glory of the Lord was settling in on me and I began to declare the supernatural presence of God, and laugh at demonic activity around me—this was an unusual service for me.

As I walked down the aisle I came upon a woman with her head bowed and her hands curled and crippled, almost completely closed in a circle. Before I knew it, the compassion of Christ came right out of my heart and moved through my own hands. I put my fingers up under the small space separating her fingers from the palms of her hands, and commanded those hands to straighten out in the name of Jesus.

I slid my hands under hers and her fingers began to straighten out until they were completely opened. At my direction, she slowly but firmly opened and closed her hands with ease, totally released by the Holy Spirit's power. I remember rejoicing at the spontaneous flow of Christ's compassion, His power to set her free!

The compassion of Jesus is a mighty force to be reckoned with. In this generation that has been discarded and cast aside by parents, spouses, and church folk, God wants to express His heart again. He wants to love others through His people again. God desires to see His sons and daughters walking around and reaching out to people just as Jesus did on this earth.

Now is the time to get on our faces before the Lord and cry out to Him to take away every bit of pride, arrogance, and selfish ambition from our hearts. Let us ask Him to replace any self-centeredness with a fire from the altar of His glory. May we have a fresh encounter with the love, mercy, and goodness of the Father; and may we begin to release it upon those who live in darkness around us.

As we walk with the heart of Jesus into the marketplaces, the government halls, the school systems, and the communities that surround us, His compassion for hurting people will automatically tie us into and allow us to partner with God's supernatural power, for the healing and deliverance of this generation.

Now, let's enjoy some of those power stories of God's miraculous compassion as told by my father. You will see how God's compassion works through the prayers of family members and friends—and how His compassion can reach across the air channels of radio. Be encouraged! There is no limit to the miracle-working power of the compassion of Jesus Christ!

CHAPTER 7

COMPASSION-DRIVEN MIRACLE STORIES

as told by R. W. Schambach

BROKEN NEEDLES AND A PHONE CALL

Back in the 1960s, I rented a synagogue in Philadelphia, and I held a revival there for two weeks. While I was there, an elderly woman came to see me about her son, who was hooked on drugs. She said, "He has come into the house and stolen every light. He stole the couch. He stole the rugs. My house is bare! He took it all and sold it to pump into his arm!"

When you're hooked on drugs, you're going to find it somewhere. If you used to be a drug addict (or still are one), you know what I'm talking about. You'll find it somewhere.

She said, "I can't get him to church."

"He doesn't have to come to church," I told her. Then I laid hands on her and prayed the same prayer that I prayed for Brother Price in Newark. "Holy Ghost, sic him!"

After I prayed, the Lord gave me a prophetic word for the woman. "Go on home. Your son is delivered."

You might say, "Well, anyone could have said that to her." But I was operating under the anointing of the Holy Ghost. He doesn't lie! So I knew that her son was delivered.

I came back to the synagogue the next night. The same lady had come back to the service. This time she had a young man with her. She got my attention. This young man had a story to tell. There's always a story to tell. Hallelujah!

The night before he had been in an alley with a needle, trying to give himself a shot, when the needle broke. But drug addicts are used to that. They always carry a spare in their billfold. So he pulled the spare out and tried to inject it into his arm. Then that needle broke!

He had to have a quick fix, so he went to his pusher's apartment. (Now from what I'm told, that's a no-no!)

He beat on the door. The guy opened the door.

"What are you doing at my house?" he said. "Get in here!"

"Man, I need a quick fix," the young man told him. "I got the drugs from you earlier, but I broke two needles. Get me a needle. I need a shot now."

So the pusher went to get him another needle.

What this young man told me next thrilled me. Right there in the pusher's apartment, something left him. He suddenly had no cravings for the drug. Right there in front of the pusher, a miracle took place!

The pusher tried to force it on him. "Here's the needle. Give yourself—"

"No, wait. I don't need it. Something happened; I don't know what it was."

Then he gave back the drugs he had bought earlier. Now this is another no-no for the drug addict. But he was delivered! He was set free! He didn't need them anymore.

That night, his mama was coming home from church. If you've ever been to our meetings, you know they are a little lengthy. She was getting back to her house around midnight. To her surprise, her son showed up. This was early for him. He never came in before two, three, or four o'clock in the morning. (It didn't matter. He didn't have a bed anyway. He had stolen it and sold it already.)

When his mama saw him coming up the steps, she said, "What are you doing home so early?"

He said, "Mother, I don't know. Something happened to me tonight." And he told her the story I told you.

"Oh!" she said. "Brother Schambach laid hands on me and sent the Word to you and commanded that devil to turn you loose. That monkey is off your back right now!"

Oh, hallelujah! He was in the service that night and got saved, sanctified, and filled with the Holy Ghost.

PROXY

There was another lady who came to me one time. She said, "Oh, Brother Schambach. I have a daughter who ran away from home, and I don't know where she is. I haven't heard from her for six years."

And I said, "God will do it." Then I prayed that same prayer. "Holy Ghost, sic her! Knock her down where she is! Bring her to the foot of the cross. And tonight, make her dial her mother's phone number."

When I got done, I looked at that woman and said, "Go home and sit by the phone. You're going to get a call from your daughter."

She came back the next night shouting and jumping. She had a great testimony. She said, "Brother Schambach, it was just like you said. When I got home, I sat by the phone. My daughter called me for the first time in six years. She said, 'I don't know why I'm calling you, but something got hold of me.' I said, 'That's the Holy Ghost!'"

This is proxy! You can believe for somebody else. God knows what to do. If He can find two of us here on earth agreeing, as touching anything, that they shall ask and it shall be done.

Are you ready to see that loved one set free? Well, you're going to put your faith to work. You're going to stand proxy for him or her, and God's going to give you the miracle that you've been praying for. Let's pray, shall we?

> *Father, in the name of Jesus, we ask that You touch the life of lost loved ones right now. Put a hook in their jaw and drag them to the foot of Calvary. Arrest them in their tracks. Get hold of them, in Jesus' name. Save them and fill them with the Holy Ghost. We thank You for Your miracle-working power. We ask this in the name of Jesus. Amen and amen.*

VOICE OF POWER

I love ministering to people through radio broadcasts. I've been on radio for many years now. There's just something about it. You see, when people hear a broadcast, they can't sit back and judge the preacher because of the way he looks or acts. They can't sit back and say, "Well, I don't like his tie. I don't like his suit. I don't like him!"

They can only judge a preacher by what he says. So when I preach on radio, people can only judge me by the Word of God that I bring forth, not by how I dress or what color I am. In fact, many people think I'm a black preacher!

God has saved and delivered so many people through the "Voice of Power" broadcast. I have three testimonies that I want to share of people who were at the end of their ropes—at the point of suicide—when they heard an old-fashioned Holy Ghost preacher on their radio. God delivered them.

There was a gentleman in Boston who seemed like he had it all. He was a successful businessman. He had a new house, a new car, and a fine family. But he had one downfall—he was an alcoholic. This tore his family apart. It cost him his job, and eventually his family left him.

"I couldn't afford milk for my baby," he later testified, "but I still bought the booze."

He soon lost his house, too. The last day he was there, he sat alone in the empty house (the furniture was already gone). He figured that he might as well end it all there. He planned to commit suicide.

He turned up the radio as loud as it would go so his neighbors wouldn't hear the gun go off when he shot himself. Just as he was about to pull the trigger, he heard a voice on the radio. It was the voice of a loud, Pentecostal preacher who singled him out.

"Don't touch that dial! Suicide is not your answer! Put your hand on the radio right now, and I'll pray for that spirit of oppression and suicide to leave you."

Immediately, he went to his radio, cradled it in his arms, and prayed that prayer with me. Right there in that empty house, he gave his life to Christ and was instantly delivered from alcoholism.

He got his family back and found an even better job than the one he had lost. In just two years, he was able to pay for a new home as well.

MONTGOMERY

Another man God delivered through radio was a brother named Montgomery, who had been a pastor. After his church split, he had left the ministry and went into construction.

His church wasn't the only thing that split. He and his wife went through a divorce. His life was falling apart piece by piece.

One morning, a spirit of oppression swept over him, urging him to commit suicide. He tried to stand up against it, but nothing worked. He wanted to kill himself.

That night, he fell into bed and cried out, "God, I put myself in Your care."

God answered him, "Son, I'm sending a prophet." Of course, Montgomery had no idea what that meant, but at three o'clock in the morning, he turned on the radio in desperation. The "Voice of Power" broadcast was on. At the end of the message, he heard the same kind of charge that the man from Boston had heard.

"Don't turn off your radio. I'm going to pray for someone very specifically...that young preacher who has been tormented by a spirit of suicide today. You foul spirit, I curse you in the name of the Lord Jesus." As soon as I spoke those words, the oppression left instantly and never returned.

THE FAMILY

The final story is one that came across my desk many years ago from Canada.

There was a family of two parents and three daughters. They were facing a crisis time financially; no one in the household was able to find a job to meet their needs. They literally could not put food on the table.

A heavy depression settled in on the father and spread to the entire family. He and his wife decided it would be better if they all died together, right now, instead of waiting for starvation. So the family formed a suicide pact. They planned to end it all in their garage, inhaling the carbon monoxide fumes.

When the day arrived, they took their places in the car. The father started the car, but then the mother reached across and shut off the ignition.

"What if we wait just one more day?" she pleaded.

Angrily, the father jumped out of the car. If his wife persisted, he would lose his nerve. He hoped he would be able to get back in the car tomorrow.

In his anger, he went in the house and started kicking things around. Finally, he turned on the radio. The radio man was new to him, but what the preacher was saying captured his attention. The preacher was talking about a demon of suicide that convinces people there's no hope. "Mister, suicide is not the answer to your problems. Jesus Christ is the only answer."

This was the first time the father had heard about Jesus, who not only could save a life from sin, but was able to deliver from all kinds of oppression, including thoughts of suicide.

The entire family realized that a tormenting spirit was trying to destroy their lives and send them to hell. On their knees in the living room, the entire family repented of their sins and received Jesus as Lord of their home.

Within days, God turned their situation around.

CHAPTER 8

KEY #4: AUTHORITY

Donna Schambach

I had been living in Tyler, Texas, for well over ten years, serving my father in ministry. All of Dad's kids were grown, my brothers having adult children of their own.

We all had grown up in a household of faith. The only time we saw a doctor as children was when it was required by law for entrance to school, or in extreme emergency situations. Always, our first recourse was to approach our Great Physician, and call on Him in the time of sickness. When Dad was home, he usually laid hands on us and that settled the issue.

One day in Tyler, my parents received an unusual call from my sister-in-law. My brother Bob was running a high fever with acute pain in his side that seemed to be getting worse with each passing moment. They were taking him to the emergency room.

Dad and Mother quickly drove to the hospital and arrived just in time to lay hands on Bob. Dad didn't walk into the room with a lot of fanfare; he simply commanded the pain to cease and the fever to go in the name of Jesus.

Just after prayer, we learned the doctors were planning to remove Bob's appendix, believing it was near rupturing. But when they came back into the room to check his vitals, his temperature had dropped to normal and the pain was quickly subsiding. The surgeon came in to poke on his side—no pain.

"Mr. Schambach, I cannot explain what just happened. When an appendix gets that bad, there is never a reversal. That's why we move so quickly to operate; we don't want the poison released into your blood stream. But the second set of X-rays show a completely normally functioning appendix. I'm going to send you home."

Bobby gave the doctor a simple explanation, "My dad just prayed for me."

Those words may mean one thing to the average listener, but the Schambach kids knew Dad had authority when he prayed. He took God at His Word; and when He prayed, the Word of God was his legal right for expecting miracles.

Anyone who functions in the supernatural with God's power flowing through them will be on the front lines confronting territorial demon spirits who are unwilling to free their victims. Those imps will resist every attempt we make to set captives free.

So, as any well-trained combatant, we need to be prepared. We must understand the authority of the kingdom we represent. We must know the document that gives us the legal right to cast out demonic squatters.

That means, we must know the Word of God. Take these words of Jesus, for instance:

Look, I have given you authority over all the power of the enemy, and you can walk among snakes and scorpions and crush them. Nothing will injure you (Luke 10:19 NLT).

It is one thing to know that Jesus delegated His authority to His disciples, giving them and us the right to act in His stead on earth. It is quite another to know what He knew.

Jesus was the living Word of God and knew every bit of the truth. Our growth in the exercise of the authority Jesus delegated, increases with our familiarity with His Word. A strong foundation in the Word is key in the anointing for miracles.

HOMESCHOOL OF FAITH

My father's foundation in the Word of God was a homeschool of faith. His mother, who had been powerfully healed of a crippling disease, started out life as a Mennonite and became a Pentecostal believer when she had a supernatural encounter with the power of God.

From that day on, Bob Schambach was rooted and grounded in the Scriptures for healing, provision, and salvation. Anna Schambach trusted God for the salvation of all her children: for the protection of her sons who went to war; for the food to feed six children in the midst of the Great Depression; and for her own personal health. She maintained a strong confession and carried herself with unshakeable faith, because her life was grounded on the Word and she vocalized it at every opportunity:

Many are the afflictions of the righteous: but the Lord delivereth him out of them all (Psalm 34:19 KJV).

And the Lord shall make thee the head, and not the tail; and thou shalt be above only, and thou shalt not be beneath; if that thou hearken unto the commandments of the Lord thy God, which I command thee this day, to observe and to do them (Deuteronomy 28:13 KJV).

> *For God hath not given us the spirit of fear; but of power, and of love, and of a sound mind* (2 Timothy 1:7 KJV).

> *Ye are of God, little children, and have overcome them: because greater is he that is in you, than he that is in the world* (1 John 4:4 KJV).

These are the Scriptures my father learned from childhood; and these are the Scriptures that rolled out of His spirit when He preached and confronted demon spirits.

Dad's grounding in the Word continued when he enrolled in Bible school for three years. Then, after two short pastorates, A. A. Allen invited him to join his evangelistic team as his afternoon speaker and general manager.

The afternoon services were another part of his grounding in the Word of God and in learning his authority over devils. Brother Allen called those afternoon services "Faith Clinics."

My father individually interviewed the people with needs for physical healing. He filled out cards with each name and their corresponding information. All week long he preached faith to those who came; and, when the evening services began, Brother Allen often called first for prayer those who filled out cards in the faith clinics.

Many miracles took place in those evening services, especially for the ones who had the Word of God pumped into their spirits during those day clinics. Dad learned firsthand, *"...faith comes by hearing, and hearing by the word of God"* (Romans 10:17).

Dad had routinely heard the Word of God from his mother, studied the Word of God in school, and preached the Word of

God day after day. The Word became a living part of him and built an *authority* into his heart to confront sickness and oppression.

I believe Dad's regular discipline of vocalizing and proclaiming the words of God released the gift of faith in him. This is the gift in which he operated most; the gift that often evoked the working of miracles and the gifts of healing. The gift of faith operated so strongly in him, it also worked in his role as "fisher of men," producing a fierce boldness in his spirit to relentlessly go after souls with the authority of Heaven.

I, too, had to learn to operate in the authority delegated to me by Christ.

As the daughter, studying Dad in the pulpit since early childhood, I often equated his boldness to confront sin, sickness, and demons to his masculinity and definitely to his calling—a calling I did not know would be mine one day.

I definitely had a strong foundation in the Word of God. My family, including parents, grandmother, aunts and uncles, were in my life strongly, constantly quoting, discussing, and preaching the Word of God to me and to each other. Our home was an incubator for the power of the Word.

Dad had a strong leading of the Lord to place his children in Christian school, and the two eldest of us landed in one of the most advanced in the nation, with instruction in theology, apologetics, and Bible memory from grade school through graduation.

All of us were in church, Sunday school, and weeks-long tent meetings, especially in the summers. One might say we were immersed in Bible truth all of our lives, thoroughly familiar with both the hearing and understanding of the Word.

Yet, that did not guarantee authority—it was only a strong basis for it. Authority from the Word comes first through revelation of its power, and then by our usage of it in the times we confront the enemy.

WORKING THE WORD

My first experience with "working" the Word came my last year of high school. I remember it vividly. I was a cheerleader and my school's varsity basketball team was having an undefeated season. We were at the end of the year and heading into tournaments. The outcome of those games would determine the championship of our league.

Two days before the huge tournament, I came down with the flu. I was vomiting nonstop and had a high fever. The night before the opening game, both my parents told me they were sorry but I was not going to the games. I was weak and could not steady myself on my own two feet.

As you can imagine, I was extremely disappointed and I lay in bed with tears pouring out of my eyes. I felt so sick and weak. Then a thought occurred to me, *Why don't I put my faith to work for healing?*

Up until this time I was used to my father being the one to always intercede for my healing when I became sick. He would lay his hands on me and God would do the rest.

This time was different. I really believe God was allowing me to be in a position to learn how to use His Word.

No one told me what to do next; I just spoke to God silently, "Tomorrow, Lord, when I throw my legs over this bed to get up, I believe I will be healed. I believe by Your stripes, I am healed." Nothing in the natural supported that conclusion. I still had a fever and was extremely weakened. The words came out of my spirit.

The next day I swung my feet over the bed and placed them on the floor, saying out loud, "By Your stripes, I am healed. Thank You for healing me, Lord Jesus."

I stood up on both feet and felt much stronger than the day before. Next, I headed for the shower and then to get dressed. Each step brought new strength, so eventually I entered the kitchen to ask my grandmother to make me something to eat. I believe she said something like, "You are still not going to that game tonight."

Knowing better than to argue with my grandmother, I just waited it out. And, by the time evening came, I was visibly stronger. The fever was gone and I was keeping food down.

I asked my parents again if I could go to the game. I promised them I would not overdo it. And, surprisingly, they let me go.

All evening long I was jumping, cheering, and doing cartwheels. No one would have guessed I had been so sick. I came home from the game completely well, strong, and extremely happy about our team's victory.

Some might think it was a case of mind over matter, but I knew differently. I knew how I felt. No positive thinking would have gotten me out of bed. God honored my faith and honored my connection with His Word.

When I reflect on this instant healing in my life, I also clearly see the Holy Spirit's role in it. He prompted my thinking. He helped me set a point of contact for my faith, believing as soon as my feet hit the floor I would be healed. And, He helped me remember this Scripture to encourage my faith:

> *But He was wounded for our transgressions, He was bruised for our iniquities; the chastisement for our peace*

was upon Him, and by His stripes we are healed (Isaiah 53:5).

The Holy Spirit makes the Word of God "alive" to us—He causes each verse to light up like a flashing neon sign in our hearts. When we grasp His signal to believe, miracles take place. Each believer who learns to put the words of the Bible to work for health and healing, will gain a new "authority"—the authority of the Word of God Himself to conquer the enemy's advances in every arena of life.

Be encouraged today. Faith is a life-long process of learning, and we don't always get it right.

I remember when I first moved to the Bronx in New York to start a Christian school. The pastor of the church for whom I worked also asked me to be part of his pastoral staff and he sometimes asked me to teach or preach.

When people heard that Donna "Schambach" was in town, I guess they expected me to be just like my father. I wasn't even close.

One day I received an invitation from a church member to come to her home for a home-cooked Italian meal, one offer I never turned down in our Bronx neighborhood with a huge Italian-American population. I was excited to accept.

I soon learned that my hostess had a hidden agenda. On the couch sat a woman over six feet tall, who looked like she might have come from the Caribbean Islands. She had no expression on her face and was absolutely mute. She loomed like a human skyscraper; a person with whom I would never want to tangle.

My hostess brought me into the room where her other houseguest sat and told me the woman was demon-possessed. She let me know I was to cast the devil out of the woman before dinner.

I must confess, I wondered why my hostess hadn't prepared me beforehand. I knew well how inexperienced I was at casting out devils. I had only seen it done by the big leaguers, and this was pretty serious, not to mention, scary stuff. The woman on the couch looked very intimidating.

But, I didn't usually back down from a challenge, so I took a deep breath and started praying.

I prayed in the Holy Spirit. I used the words I heard Dad use when he was casting out devils: "In the name of Jesus!" "I take authority over you, devil!" "Come out!" "Be gone!"

You name it, I said it. I named every demon I could possibly command. I continued to take "authority" in the name of Jesus. I pounded on her back and took her face in my hands, commanding the devil to look me in my eyes and listen to me.

Nothing happened. No sound. No movement. The woman never blinked. If she had demons, and I believed she had many, they weren't budging that day. I couldn't beat them out. I couldn't even get a rise out of them.

I, on the other hand, was sweating, angry, and feeling totally defeated. When I went into the kitchen to eat spaghetti, I couldn't enjoy it. As soon as politely possible, I left my friends and that very delicious Italian meal, feeling like an utter failure.

Thankfully, God wasn't finished training me yet.

About a year later, I had been spending some time in prayer during the day before our church's midweek service. An unusual spirit of intercession came over me, and I felt as though God had a specific person in mind.

When I walked into church, I arrived a little late, so I sat on the back row.

The pastor called people to move forward for prayer and, all of a sudden, a woman on the far left began to scream and wail. I instinctively looked up and my pastor gave me the nod to go over and pray with her.

As I approached her, all I did was put my arm across her shoulder and whisper in her ear, "I take authority over you, you lying spirit."

Instantly, the woman released a blood-curdling scream and fell hard against the floor. I knew she had been set free from a deceptive, lying devil that had been tormenting her; she arose from the floor a new person.

I soon began to understand how much simpler the Lord's work could be when I learned to hear and yield to the promptings of the Holy Spirit. (This topic is discussed in more depth in following chapters.)

One time He may put a Scripture in my heart to stand upon and confess; another time He may put a command in my mouth to address a spirit of which He is aware. I am simply an emissary of the Lord Jesus Christ. I function by His Spirit with the authority of His Word.

A SET-APART LIFESTYLE

One final comment is necessary here. As servants of the Lord Jesus, we do not only *use* the authority of His Word, but we are required to *live* by the authority of His Word. The release of holy authority through our lives is directly related to our commitment to our living holy and practicing a "set-apart" lifestyle.

I remember an older gentleman in the ministry encouraging me about the call he saw on my life. He said some astonishing things, and his final words to me were, "But Donna, no foolishness! No foolishness!"

Immediately I knew what he meant. The call on my life required a set apart lifestyle. I had already been learning that I had to put television and conversation aside when I was preparing to minister. Often times it felt as though I was missing out on what others enjoyed; but I had to have a quiet heart in order to hear from the Lord.

I also knew I could not harbor any secret sins. In my life, I needed people who knew my strengths and weaknesses and were willing to hold me accountable. I needed prayer warriors and intercessors to stand with me. My life had to be one of continual examination and repentance, because the Holy Spirit wanted a prepared vessel.

When we are people of the Word, we will live by its authority. The Word will rule our hearts. The Word is true:

> *How can a young man cleanse his way? By taking heed according to Your word. With my whole heart I have sought You; oh, let me not wander from Your commandments! Your word I have hidden in my heart, that I might not sin against You"* (Psalm 119:9-11).

> *Your word is a lamp to my feet and a light to my path* (Psalm 119:105).

Make no mistake; the enemy knows when we live our lives from relationship with the Word of God—and when we are just going through the motions.

All the huffing, puffing, prancing, and performing we might attempt only reduce us to paper tigers if we are not backed up with the weightiness of the Word of God in our lives.

Remember this: Jesus, after fasting forty days and nights, in a weakened physical condition, defeated satan in the wilderness. He didn't do it through physical exertion or cunning speech, He simply used the sword of the Spirit, the Word of God—and He promptly disposed of His enemy. "It is written," Jesus declared three times, and the devil left him.

The Word is the authority for our lives and mission, just as it was for Jesus and His ministry. The more we are able to use the Word of God within our hearts as a mighty sword to defeat every lying advance of the enemy, the more we will walk in new degrees of authority and partnership with God's supernatural power.

I can testify my father walked in the authority of the Word of God, both in his personal life and in his ministry. In the next chapter are more powerful miracle stories, told by him, that are an outworking of that authority on His life. Remember, you can walk in the authority of Christ too, as the Word becomes part of you and is activated in your walk and talk.

CHAPTER 9

MIRACLES OF AUTHORITY

as told by R. W. Schambach

SHARON'S NEW EYE MIRACLE

My wife and I pastored a church in the early 1950s. A man, who later became a dear friend of mine, used to bring his 6-year-old daughter to Sunday school. He would always drop her off, and I would wonder who her parents were. But he would never come to Sunday school. He would never come to church.

One day I jumped in front of his car to stop him. I wanted to talk to him. But he knew who I was, and that was the last time I jumped in front of his car. He put it in gear and laid the rubber down. I flew into the bushes. He didn't want to talk to the preacher.

I was after that big fish. I liked that little girl coming to Sunday school, but I wanted the father to come also. However, he couldn't bring himself to come to church. I knew he was a sinner. Sinners don't like to go to church.

One day my wife and I were on vacation visiting her mother in Philadelphia. I got a long-distance phone call. I heard a strange voice on the other end of the line. The man had tears in his voice. He said, "Brother Schambach?"

I said, "Who is this?" It was that little girl's father. I said, "Oh, something must be wrong. You called me brother. You tried to run over me last time we met. What's wrong?"

He said, "I am in the hospital in McKeesport, Pennsylvania."

I said, "What is wrong with you?"

"Nothing is wrong with me. It is my daughter."

That daughter was the apple of her daddy's eye. "What happened?" I asked.

He told me that his family was visiting them. While the children were playing in the backyard, her cousin picked up a rusty nail and threw it. It was an accident, but it hit his daughter in the eye and shattered the eyeball. The doctors wanted to cut the eye out.

"Well," I said, "let them operate."

He said, "She told me to call you!"

I said, "What would you like me to do?" I wanted him to lay it on the line.

"She wants you to come and bring that bottle of oil. She says that if you pray for her, everything will be all right."

Kids have faith! "Well," I said, "I am thankful she wants me to come. I am her pastor. What about you?"

He said, "Please come."

I replied, "I am on the way. Don't let the doctors operate. Don't let them do anything until I get there." I took the next plane out.

I had visited that hospital practically every day in the past. Doctors there knew me on a first name basis. I would pray and minister to the sick. Two of the young interns met me at the entrance. They said, "Hurry up and do your thing. An infection is setting in the eye. We have to take her to the operating room and remove the eye."

I said, "Now, hold on, fellows. What makes you think that after I do my thing you are going to have to do your thing? That is why I have been called. That girl is expecting a miracle!"

Children believe God. I would rather lay hands on a child than on an adult any day. It is the adults I have problems with. Children believe anything you tell them. The adults, however, deal with logic all the time. They want to know what makes it work. They want to logically figure it out. That is why adults often get nothing from God. A child just says, "Pray for me, and I will be all right."

The interns said, "We aren't going to argue with you. Go in anyway."

I didn't go in the room. I headed for the waiting room because I knew her father would be there. I wasn't about to go in and pray for that girl. I wanted that man first. He wasn't going to run over me anymore.

There he was. He was weeping. His daughter was suffering.

I said, "I finally caught up with you. Get on your knees. It is time to pray now."

The two doctors came in and said, "Will you please come with us? The trouble isn't here, it is inside."

I answered, "That is why you are a doctor and not a preacher. You don't even know where the trouble is. I have been after this guy for about nine months. I am not about to let this fish go now. Get on your knees, brother. We are getting right with God."

I didn't have to beg him. He fell on his face. He prayed, and we touched God. God saved him and gave him a miracle in his life. After God transformed him, I said, "Let's go now." We headed for Sharon's room. I will never forget her. She was a pretty little blond girl. There she was, lying on her bed with a patch over her eye. When I stepped in, she turned to me and smiled. "I knew you would come," she said softly. "Everything is all right now."

I got out my bottle of oil and walked toward her. There were two doctors standing next to me. They said, "What are you doing?" I got my bottle out and put oil on her. They were looking at the oil saying, "Can I look at that? What is this, holy oil?"

I said, "No. I got it from my wife's kitchen. She fries chicken in it. I bought it at the A & P. There isn't anything holy about the oil. Oil can't heal you. You can go swim in oil and it won't heal you."

And the prayer offered in faith will make the sick person well; the Lord will raise them up. And if they have sinned, they will be forgiven (James 5:15 NIV).

There is something about a child who just believes God. I didn't want to answer all those questions, so I said to the doctors, "Please wait outside, will you? Wait until I get done. You don't let me in your operating room, so please step out of mine."

They went out. I didn't even bother to look at the eye. I didn't have to look at it—I wasn't the doctor. I laid hands on her and said a simple prayer. I didn't even shake. I said, "Father, in the name of Jesus, perform the miracle and give her a new eye." That is all I said. I turned to the door and saw the two doctors. I waved for them to come in.

They asked, "Can we have her now, Reverend?" They were getting testy with me now. They had never called me reverend before.

I said, "What are you going to do with her?"

"Well, we told you the eye is infected. We have to cut it out."

I said, "It isn't infected anymore."

"What are you talking about?"

I said, "Didn't you tell me that the eye was shattered in a hundred pieces? You said that. I never even looked at it."

"Why, of course, that is why we have to operate."

I said, "You don't have to take her anymore. God just performed a miracle." I knew that little girl had faith. I knew God wasn't going to disappoint that faith. He never disappoints faith.

They said, "What do you mean?"

I said, "Look at the eye."

They went over, took the bandage off, and took a peek at it.

"I don't believe it!" the doctors exclaimed.

I said, "That is the reason I had you stand outside the door. You can't believe it even when you look at it."

Jesus said, *"Blessed is she who believed, for there will be a fulfillment of those things which were told her from the Lord"* (Luke 1:45).

God is looking for men and women who will stand on His Word believing that if He said it, He will do it, and that if He spoke it, He will bring it to pass. God has to take you outside that human realm in order to do something supernatural.

MAN WRAPPED IN SHEET

I was preaching in Houston, Texas, when a woman walked into my meeting with a sheet on her shoulder. I wondered what she had in that sheet. It wasn't long before I found out, because she walked down the center aisle and dropped it at my feet. I was preaching— she was messing up my service! When she opened the sheet, there was a man in it—her husband. He weighed only 58 pounds.

She said, "My husband used to weigh 200 pounds." Now he looked like a human skeleton. The stench of the man's disease almost knocked me out. I knew it was cancer. The woman looked at me and said, "It took me all night to get here, preacher. Now do what God called you to do. Heal this man."

These are the types of situations that help you find out whether you are called and sent, or whether you just went.

The woman said, "I come from New Orleans. The doctor told me yesterday my husband has seventy-two hours to live. One of those days is already shot. That means we only have forty-eight hours. When the doctor told me the news, I told him I was taking my husband to Houston. He told me there was no use in taking him to Houston. He thought I wanted to bring him here to the cancer specialists, and he said they would give me the same bottom line—that my husband is going to die. I just told the doctor, 'That's what you think.'"

That is the truth about faith, isn't it? Sometimes you have to stand alone.

The doctor told her he wouldn't let her move the patient, but she said, "He is my husband. I will sign him out." That is the kind of woman to have. Most women would try to get rid of the old rascal. But she said, "He is my man. I am not going to let that devil have him."

The doctor said, "Those specialists are going to give you the same diagnosis I did."

She said, "I am not taking him to a specialist. I am taking him to a man of God."

He said, "A what?"

"A man of God."

He said, "I don't believe in that."

She said, "You don't have to. He is my man. I believe in it. That is the bottom line."

Let every person, let every devil be a liar, but let God be true! If He said it, He will do it, and if He spoke it, He will bring it to pass!

She said, "I am going to sign him out."

The doctor said, "I will hide his clothes."

She said, "I will steal a sheet."

I looked at the sheet, and it had the name of the hospital on it. She had stolen it! Faith never gives up. Faith will find a way. Faith presses on. Faith takes the answer from God. Faith never sits in a pew. Faith steps out on the water. Faith steps out on the Word. Faith says, "Yes, Lord, I am going to take the answer." God can't lie. I believe what He said.

She said, "Brother Schambach, let's dispense with the talking now. Lay your hands on him."

I couldn't stand to look at him because the stench was coming right at my face. I had to turn my face, but I touched him. I said,

"You foul devil. I curse you at the roots in the name of Jesus, and I command you to die and pass from this man's body."

The man was only in his late forties. The devil kills people before their time. The thief comes to steal, to kill, to destroy. I could see the marks of the devil on that body, but I refused to let the devil have him. I said, "In the name of Jesus, I reverse it." I threw the sheet on him and said, "Get him out of here. He is well."

He didn't get up and walk. He only weighed 58 pounds—skin and bones. The woman picked him up, threw him right back over her shoulder, walked out, didn't even stay for the offering. Halfway back, she turned around and said, "Bye, Brother Schambach. See you when you get to New Orleans."

Six months later we put the tent up in New Orleans. During the opening night, I saw a big man enter. He was six-feet-one and weighed 200 pounds. He wore a brand-new blue suit. I didn't know who he was. He walked up on the ramp, and I wondered why my men let him get up there. The Holy Ghost must have frozen them right in their spot. We don't let anybody up on the platform. All of a sudden, this guy grabbed me and lifted me off the ground. I said, "Put me down."

He said, "I am the man who was in the sheet."

I said, "Pick me back up again. Let's dance!"

Isn't that beautiful? Six months later, he was back to his normal weight. He hadn't even known his wife had taken him to Houston. He was just about gone, forty-eight hours to live. When she took him back to the doctor, they examined him and couldn't find a trace of cancer anywhere.

When I spoke to that cancer, I spoke resurrection life into his body. I spoke to that mountain. I spoke in faith believing God was going to do it. I called it done. If God says He is the Healer, I have a right to pronounce him healed. Speak it into existence in the name of Jesus.

For we do not wrestle against flesh and blood, but against principalities, against powers, against the rulers of the darkness of this age, against spiritual hosts of wickedness in the heavenly places (Ephesians 6:12).

Five of you shall chase a hundred, and a hundred of you shall put ten thousand to flight; your enemies shall fall by the sword before you (Leviticus 26:8).

WHY?

You are of God, little children, and have overcome them, because He who is in you is greater than he who is in the world (1 John 4:4).

SPIT IN MY EYES

A precious saint of God, who had been blind for thirty-eight years, was in New York city. She was standing in line ready to receive prayer. There were about 500 people to pray for—and the ushers brought her first. After I prayed, I said, "I believe God. It is done. You are healed."

She said, "No, I am not."

I put my arm to her back and I tried to move her along but she just dug in. She said, "I am not going anywhere. You didn't do what God told me to tell you to do."

I said, "Take it by faith."

She said, "No." She just stayed there. She said, "Brother Scham- bach, God told me to tell you to do something. I am not leaving here until you do it."

I said, "All right, what did He tell you?"

She said, "He told me to tell you to spit in my eyes."

I said, "I am not going to do that. It isn't sanitary. It isn't healthy. I am not going to do it."

She said, "Yes, you are, because I am not leaving until you do. God told me to tell you to do this."

She wouldn't budge. I said, "I won't do it. I am not spitting on you."

She said, "Brother Schambach, I'm tired of being blind. Jesus did this to heal a blind man. Are you better than Jesus?"

She knew how to hurt a guy. I said, "I'm going to find out if God really spoke to you."

She wouldn't give up. Thank God for women who don't give up. Don't you take no for an answer. If you find something in the Book, stick by your guns. Say, "Devil, you are a liar." Show your faith to God. Say, "God, look what You said here. You can't lie. If You said it, then it belongs to me. I'm going to write my name right there on the side of the margin, 'Lord, it belongs to me.'"

The woman refused to give up. She knew God's voice. I began to weep. But I did what God had told her should be done. And the moment I did, the power of God hit her. For the first time in thirty-eight years, 20-20 vision came back to her eyes. She ran around the building!

Don't give up. Don't ever give up! Whatever He says for you to do, do it. God is looking for obedience.

CHAPTER 10

KEY #5: OBEDIENCE

Donna Schambach

When we study the life of Jesus, we quickly learn He not only spent much time with the Father to receive instruction, but He immediately and carefully obeyed everything the Father asked Him to do.

No matter how childlike His faith or compassionate His heart, Jesus would have seen no miracles if He was not willing to obey His Father. Obedience opens the door for the finger of God to work.

(If Dad had not been willing to obey when the lady asked him to spit in her eyes, the eyes may have never opened. He had to lose his pride, humble himself, and go with the prompting of the Spirit to see that amazing miracle that day.)

I, too, have struggled with obedience in the pulpit from time to time. Often the struggle stems from my not wanting to be embarrassed. It is a foolish mistake for a servant of God to be so focused on herself that she misses what God wants to do for the needs of the people.

For a period of a few years we held schools of ministry in our hometown, several different weeks throughout the year. We offered day sessions for the students and evening camp meeting-style services at night. My assignment for the camp meeting was to preach the opening service.

During that particular time, I was a strong support to my aging parents and traveled as little as possible so I could be close to home in case they needed me. Often during those times, I struggled with feelings of hopelessness with regard to the call on my life. I felt out of touch with God's purpose and wondered if future ministry would be limited because I could not invest in it the way I thought I should.

So when I did stand at the podium, I had to listen closely to the voice of the Lord. Usually I was quite sure about the message God gave me for the people, but as I brought the message to a close, I sometimes struggled.

Camp meetings, for the most part, were believers' rallies. Those who came were hungry for learning and for a move of God. I didn't expect many nonbelievers to attend. So when the Holy Spirit prompted me to give an altar call, I often heard a contrary voice in my head say something like, *You don't need to do that tonight; everyone is already saved. You can go on to the prayer for the sick and get the service over with. People are tired and want to go home.*

I knew that voice, too—the voice of the enemy. He hates altar calls. Although there was an initial struggle, I had learned by this time the presentation of the Gospel and the time of invitation were the most important parts of the service. Somehow I would always plow through the resistance and invite people to the front.

One particular Tuesday night I remember delivering a very stern message of conviction and repentance. The message was clear and the call to the altar was strong. The precious Holy Spirit was doing His work in spite of me. Neither my place in life nor all my insecurities mattered to Him. All He had asked for was my obedience.

So many people came forward that night, crying out to God and weeping. I was rejoicing to see the Spirit of God touch His people, but no one in particular stood out to me. I just saw a group of people praying.

BACKSLIDDEN SON

Months later, I received a letter at the office. A woman wrote to me from Shreveport, Louisiana. She wrote to thank me for my "obedience" to the Lord, and then she told me a sobering story.

Her son had been backslidden for well over a year. Every time she invited him to church he refused her because he wanted to hang out with his friends. The mama didn't argue, but she did keep praying for her son.

One spring day she received our announcement of the camp meeting and prayed her son would go. As usual, she asked him and he refused. Then a last minute surprise—the son told her he would ride with her to Tyler because all of his friends were busy and he had no one to hang with.

The mama told me they arrived a little late and sat on the back row. As the sermon was going forth, she knew God had her son in the service for the specific message He had given me that night. By the time I gave the altar call, the son practically sprinted to the altar.

At the altar, the young man fell on his face weeping, trembled uncontrollably, and fell to his knees. His mama told me he rolled back and forth across the floor. She knew God was dealing with him and setting her son free. When he came back to his seat, he put his arms around Mama and asked for forgiveness. He was forever changed.

As I read her words my own tears were falling, and then I read the last part of the letter:

"This is what I want you to know, Sister Donna. Just a few short weeks after that meeting, my son was killed in an automobile accident. Your message prepared him to meet God. I am forever grateful for your obedience that night."

The gravity hitting my heart that day is beyond description. I thought about how close I might have been to not giving an altar call that night—to giving into the enemy's lies and ignoring the voice of the Spirit—to that young man missing his time to repent.

The importance of my obeying God was underscored in my heart that day. I was determined to listen closely and carefully obey from that day forward.

Obeying God can be a challenge when God asks us to do something we don't want to do; but, obeying Him, is the key to our miracle. As you know by now, Dad witnessed outstanding healing miracles, but he also witnessed some amazing financial miracles too. Read the following wonderful testimonies, as only he can relate!

CHAPTER 11

MIRACLES REQUIRING GREAT OBEDIENCE

by R. W. Schambach

THE BACK RENT BLUES

One night at a crusade meeting, a lady walked down the aisle of the big auditorium. Tears were streaming down her face. She was holding a long sheet of paper.

There were 1,500 to 2,000 people in the audience, and everybody was being blessed but her. She was weeping desperately, grieving so deeply that it kind of grew over the whole congregation.

She said, "Brother Schambach, they are going to put me out of my house. I am four months behind in my rent." She held up the paper. "This is a notice of eviction. Tomorrow morning at ten o'clock, they are going to move everything out to the sidewalk."

I jumped off that platform and said, "Woman, the devil is a liar. They are not putting you out on the sidewalk. You are a child of God."

She said, "What about this notice?"

I took it, tore it up, and threw it under the platform. "That is your problem. You are looking at the circumstances. If you continue to do that, you will not have faith. You have to start looking in the Bible.

And my God shall supply all your need according to His riches in glory by Christ Jesus (Philippians 4:19).

The reason sick people can't get healed is that they are too busy looking at their diseases. The more they look at them, the worse they feel. We need to keep our eyes on the Word.

I did my best to encourage this woman's faith. She was weeping vehemently.

She said, "Brother Schambach, my blind mama lives with me, and all I can see is my blind mother sitting on the step."

I said, "Shut up! You are getting to me now, woman!" *(I guess that's why I'm not pastoring anymore.)* The devil is not going to put you out on the sidewalk. Sit down in that front row and listen to me preach."

I have never seen such anxiety in an individual. I had a sermon prepared but didn't use it. I left all those people, jumped down to where she was, and I preached to that woman for a solid hour. She needed it. I didn't even receive the offering until I finished preaching. Then, when I finished preaching, I went to her and said, "It is time to receive the offering."

She almost fainted. She looked up at me and said, "Don't you remember me? I need money."

I said, "I know it. Where is your pocketbook?"

She said, "But I need—"

I knew she needed money. I am a good listener. She told me she was four months behind in the rent. She also said, "I gave the man $50, but he threw it back at me because it wasn't nearly enough." I had heard that part. I knew she had $50.

I asked, "Where is your purse?"

She said, "Mama has it." Her blind mother was in the service.

I said, "Get it. You are going to give something to God."

She got mad at me. You can tell when folks get mad. But I stayed sweet because I knew she was going to be glad all over again. I was showing her the way to deliverance, and she didn't know it. I said, "We don't have much time. It is ten o'clock at night. At ten o'clock in the morning, they are coming to evict you. You do what I tell you to do, woman."

I could have taken the money out of the church treasury, and I could have paid her rent. But then she would have owed it to God, because that is God's money.

I thought, *Why not just put your faith to work and let her receive a blessing? When God blesses her with it, she will have to pay the tithe and everyone will be blessed.* This is how God works!

The woman got up in a huff and went to the back to get her purse. I saw her coming and turned my back to her as I was holding the bucket. I didn't know whether she was going to hit me with her purse or what. I didn't even want to see what she put in.

But I had challenged her to give, and she gave. When it came time for prayer, I said, "I want your blind mama first in that line." Her blind mother was indeed the first in line. I said to the woman, "Stand behind her." Then, I called the prayer line. I laid hands on

500 or 600 people that night, including the blind woman. I rebuked the blind spirit. Her eyes didn't come open suddenly. Sometimes God does it suddenly, instantly, immediately—but sometimes the healing is gradual. Yet in my spirit, I knew God had healed her.

I told her, "Mother, will you do what I tell you to do?"

She said, "Anything you say, I will do it." What a difference between her and her daughter.

I said, "Mama, I want you to go home tonight saying nothing but 'Thank You, Jesus, for giving me 20/20 vision.' Keep thanking Him until your head hits the pillow. You will wake up with perfect sight."

She said, "I will do it." She started down the ramp and said, "Devil, you are a liar. I am not blind anymore. I am thanking Jesus for 20/20 vision."

I said, "Go ahead, Mama, the whole way home."

Then it was time to pray for the woman. I laid hands on her also. I prayed a very simple prayer. I said, "Lord, I don't know how You are going to do this." I don't know how He heals folks either. All I know is He does it. So I prayed, "I am asking You to perform a miracle and pay this woman's debt." Then I said to the woman, "Look at me. In the name of Jesus, I command you to go home and unpack all those bags."

She said, "How do you know I have my bags packed?"

I said, "The way you are talking, I am surprised you haven't moved."

She said, "Half of it is at my brother's house."

"Well, get it back," I answered. "You aren't going anywhere."

That was a Sunday night. On Monday night, I was getting ready to preach when the back door of the church bounced open.

This woman wasn't walking in—she was floating in. She was six feet in the air! She was halfway down the aisle when I stopped her.

"Don't you remember me?" she asked.

I said, "I know who you are. But I am not passing up this opportunity for a sermon. I want to ask you one question. Why didn't you come to church like that last night?"

We let our troubles get to us.

I said, "The way you came into this building tonight is the way you ought to come to church no matter what kind of trouble you are going through. Psalm 100:4 says, *'Enter into His gates with thanksgiving, and into His courts with praise. Be thankful to Him, and bless His name.'* I can tell by looking at you that God did something. Come down here."

She said, "This morning, I was awakened by the smell of coffee brewing, bacon frying, and homemade biscuits baking. I sat up in my bed, catching the aroma of this breakfast. I looked over into my blind mama's bed, and it was empty. I quickly threw on a robe and ran out into the kitchen. There was my mama making breakfast. She has been blind for sixteen years, brother."

She said, "Mama, what are you doing?"

Her mother said, "Brother Schambach told me I would wake up seeing this morning, and the man of God was right. You have been making my breakfast all these years. I thought I would give you the best breakfast you ever had, daughter."

The daughter said, "We didn't eat breakfast. We had church in the kitchen at eight o'clock in the morning. At ten o'clock the constable was supposed to be there. I looked up and said, 'Oh, God, if You can open Mama's eyes, You can pay the rent. Take Your time. You still have two hours.'"

That is what I call faith. I don't know whether I could have said that with only two hours left, but when God does something for you personally, you can trust Him for the next hurdle.

At 8:30 the mailman came. She thought, *Maybe this is the way God is going to do it.* She picked up and opened the six letters she had received. You know how you open the mail looking for money? But there was no money—instead she got bills! Isn't that just like the devil? Now that her faith was strong and she was trusting God for money, she got four bills. But she just laid them on the table and said, "Lord, while You are paying the rent, please catch these four bills too!"

It was nine o'clock. The phone rang. It was a call from a woman whose name she didn't even remember.

"Well, you should remember me," the lady said. "Fourteen or fifteen years ago, you loaned me some money."

"Yeah! Now I remember you." But she never thought she would get that money back.

The lady said, "Honey, I know you thought I would never pay you back. But last night something got a hold of me." The woman explained that she had been in Chicago, shopping, when an overwhelming power took hold of her and seemed to push her toward State Street. She found herself at Pacific Garden Mission, the famous ministry where Billy Sunday got saved. I have visited that place many times. It is still open, and many people get saved in that mission. But this lady had never been to a mission in her life. The Holy Ghost dragged her in, and she sat in the back seat. A man stood up behind the rostrum to give his sermon. At the close, he gave an altar call. The lady got up. The same power that had dragged her down State Street also dragged her down that aisle. She was on her knees getting saved at the altar.

This is the best part of the story as far as I am concerned. That woman not only got saved, but as she knelt there, she got a second blessing. She heard the voice of God. God said to her, "Do you remember the woman who let you borrow money fourteen years ago?"

She said, "Yes, Lord, I do remember."

God said, "I want you to pay it back. Restitution is what it is called, wherever possible."

She said, "Well, Lord, I will find out where she lives, and I will send her a check."

God said, "No check. She needs the cash, and I not only want you to pay what you owe her but also give her six percent interest for fourteen years." God is a just God, isn't He?

She said, "But Lord, I don't know how to get in touch with her."

God told her the phone number! God even knows your telephone number. He knows your deadline—and where to find you in time to meet it. He said, "She needs it by ten o'clock in the morning."

The lady who was about to be evicted went to her old friend's house, got her money, and got back a few minutes before ten o'clock. The constable was there. She put four months' back rent on the table and four months in advance. The constable tore up the notice to evict.

When the lady finished her story, I just had one question for her: "Aren't you glad you trusted God?"

Hallelujah! You don't have any trouble. All you need is faith in God!

OBEDIENCE PAYS OFF

Many years ago, I bought a theater in Brooklyn, New York. Back then, I couldn't get churches to sponsor my meetings. I was too radical. We got so many people saved, I had to buy my own building and start a church, because I surely couldn't send them to those cold, dead churches.

So I went there to raise money for the thing. If I stayed ten days, surely I could get the down payment for the building.

There was a man who desperately needed a new truck. He was driving an old piece of junk. Have you ever driven one of those things? You've got to lay hands on it before it starts, and then you have to lay hands on it to make it stop!

The first night, this man came walking down the aisle. He said, "Brother Schambach, God spoke to me."

I said, "What did God tell you to do, brother?"

"Well, I've been saving for a new truck," he said. "But every time I save, another emergency comes, and I've got to dip into that fund. Now, I have some money here that I've been saving for that truck. While you were praying, the Lord spoke to me."

"Tell me what He said, brother," I pleaded.

"Well, I've got $500 in my pocket," he said. "And God told me if I gave Him that $500, He'll give me a new truck."

I said, "Who told you that?"

"God did," he replied.

"Well, get your money out! You can't buy a new truck anywhere for $500. If God said He'll do it, He's going to do it!"

First of all, God wants you to be obedient. I want to encourage you in your own finances that God wants to bless you—everything that your hands touch. But you've got to be obedient to the word of the Lord.

So, that man turned the money loose.

The next night he came in there with an envelope that was so big it could have choked an elephant! I mean, it was huge. That's because there were twenty-six 100-dollar bills inside.

"Oh, brother," I said, "there must be a story here!"

So I gave him the microphone and he told us one of the craziest stories I've ever heard in my life!

He was driving that old wreck of a truck down the streets of Brooklyn, and God spoke to him and said, "Stop the truck! Get out of the truck and lift up the hood."

When he did, God said, "Look down by the carburetor."

Now, God wouldn't talk to me like that, because if He asked me to look for the carburetor, I'd open the trunk. I don't know where it is. I'm not mechanically inclined. But this man knew where it was.

So the man looked down under the carburetor. He said, "Am I losing my mind? I'm looking, and I don't see anything but a carburetor." So he shut the hood, got back in and started chugging back down the street. But God stopped him again.

"I told you to stop this truck and look down there by the carburetor."

So he stopped the truck and lifted the hood. He said, "Lord, I'm looking."

God said, "Look with your hand."

When he put his hand down by the carburetor, he got a hold of something that didn't belong there. It was a roll the size of an oil filter, all covered with grease. God said, "That's it. Break it off."

He broke it off. Inside that baked grease was $26,000, all in 100-dollar bills. He was able to buy a brand new truck, and had brought me the tithes from the money.

When he told his story, that whole church went wild. They started hollering, screaming and praising God. There were about a half dozen men that got up and ran out. I think they were out there looking under their carburetors!

Praise God! This man gave an offering, and the Lord saw his heart.

When you're in financial need, you think maybe God is going to talk to somebody wealthy to come and give you help. Don't ever wonder how He is going to do it, because God's just going to turn around and do it some other way. He moves in mysterious ways!

BROTHER KEITH PROVES GOD

Read with me in Mark 12:41-44 (NIV):

Jesus sat down opposite the place where the offerings were put and watched the crowd putting their money into the temple treasury. Many rich people threw in large amounts. But a poor widow came and put in two very small copper coins, worth only a few cents. Calling his disciples to him, Jesus said, "Truly I tell you, this poor widow has put more into the treasury than all the others. They all gave out of their wealth; but she, out of her poverty, put in everything—all she had to live on."

I love that story! Jesus said that this woman gave more than all of the other people who gave to the treasury.

That doesn't make any sense to the natural mind. It would seem that other people gave a lot more money than she did. But

God does His own math! All those rich people had plenty to spare. But this precious little woman gave everything she had.

God wants us to lay it all on the line. That's what this woman did, and Jesus took notice.

A brother named Keith illustrated this principle.

I was holding a crusade in Baltimore. Keith and his wife came with some friends to the day service, where they heard my daughter, Donna, preach.

During the service, someone broke into the van they had ridden in. After this, they decided to just go home rather than staying for the evening service.

But then they ran into me. While they were waiting in the lobby of a nearby hotel for the police to arrive and take their report, we crossed paths. I greeted them like I would anybody else.

After we met, God told them to stay for the evening service and hear my message.

Now, Keith and his wife only had a few dollars between them. After paying the parking fee, they had 35 cents each. They were embarrassed to put 35 cents in the offering plate, but it was all they had, so they gave it.

It wasn't only the offering that they were worried about, though. Keith and his wife were heavily invested in their own ministry at the time, a home for troubled girls. They had bills to pay but didn't see how they were going to pay them. God knew. He saw their faith as they put the little they had in the offering.

Keith made a vow to God the next day. He said, "If you bless us with some money today, I'll give what I would like to have given last night. I'll give Brother Schambach $200."

That day, they received a check in the mail for $1,750!

It didn't matter to God that they had hardly any money. What mattered to Him was their faith. He honored that faith when they were obedient to Him.

POWER PARTNER PENNAMAN

Our ministry has what we call Power Partners. Power Partners not only pray with me, but they also help the ministry financially every month. They give $25 a month, and God blesses them.

I met a black brother in New York, Brother Pennaman. I went to preach at Madison Square Garden, and he sent me a letter. I opened that letter and a $100 check fell out. I opened it again, and a $500 check dropped out. After that I shook it, but that was the end of it, except for one of the most beautiful letters I have ever read. It blessed me.

He told me, "Brother Schambach, ever since you started Power Partners, I wanted to give, but I've been on welfare. You know, when you're on welfare, you just don't have enough money for everything. But I sent you 25 cents a week. That's a dollar a month. God started to bless me. Before long, I could send you $5 a month. You were praying for me, and the folks down there at your office were praying. Then I started sending $10 a month, and finally I became a Power Partner. You sent me that pin and my Bible. Then God got me off welfare."

That's what I desire. I want to get folks off the welfare system. I want God to bless His people. Now you read this story. It will bless your soul.

This man said, "Brother Schambach, I started getting blessed. The city gave me a job managing some apartment buildings. I was making so much money that I changed from $25 a month. The blessing of God kept being poured out on me. I had more money than I knew what to do with, so I made it $50 a month."

I mean, he was blessing me now!

He said, "Brother Schambach, now I've got two apartment buildings that I'm managing for the city. I'm sending you $100 a month now. I never made so much money in all my life. This $100 check is my Power Partner pledge for the month. That $500 check—I just got so much I don't know what to do with it. Just put it anywhere you want to."

That's a man who came from the welfare system who couldn't afford to give 25 cents a week!

When you give to God first, and you make a commitment, then God is going to see that you get blessed. When you're paying your tithes, don't give God what's left. A lot of times we take the rent out. Then we pay the phone bill, then the light bill. And we say, "Lord, this is what I have left now. I'm going to give You some."

That's all wrong. No wonder you're messed up. You take God's right off the top. Say, "Lord, this belongs to You. You're first in my life." When you start giving to God what belongs to Him, you're headed for the greatest blessing of your life.

THE $600 TENT

One night during a tent revival, I told the folks, "I need one thousand people across this nation who will give me one hundred dollars, and this tent will be paid for."

I saw a grown man dressed up nicely, and I could tell that he was a preacher. He was weeping, vehemently sobbing, heading right for me. He had six $100 bills in his hand. He put them in my hand. I said, "What are you crying for, brother?"

"Oh," he said, "I'm an evangelist, and I lost my tent. I've been saving this to buy a tent. And sitting there, God told me to give my tent savings to you!"

I knew what he was going through. But I also knew that when God tells you to make a step of faith, He has a plan and a reward in mind. I said, "Is that all He told you—just to give it?"

And this young evangelist said, "No, sir. He said if I gave it, He was going to give me a tent."

I said, "Then dry the tears up, brother." I took him by the hand, and I prayed for him. I said, "Lord, don't just give him a tent, but give him the chairs that go with it. And while You're doing that, Lord, give him a brand-new organ. And while You're doing that, Lord, give him a new truck to carry it in."

The young man wasn't crying anymore. He was saying, "Yeah, Lord! May God answer the man of God's prayer!"

Six months later, that same young evangelist came and grabbed me and danced me around and said, "Thank you, preacher! Thank you for taking that money!"

I said, "I'd like to have this on record—somebody thanking me for taking an offering."

He said, "God answered your prayer. God gave me a brand-new tent with the chairs, the platform, the Hammond organ, and a brand-new truck, and it didn't cost me a dime. Thank God I obeyed His voice!"

When *you* trust God with an offering, you may not get the same return. But God knows just what you need. He responds to our faith and obedience. When we trust God even in our need, He knows how to open doors we never dreamed possible!

CHAPTER 12

KEY #6: COVETING

Donna Schambach

My first understanding of the word "covet" came from the King James Version of the Bible, and I learned it as something *not* to do. Of course, I'm speaking of the tenth Commandment found in Exodus 20, in which God specifically demanded we never covet or "strongly desire" our neighbor's house, spouse, employees, animals, or anything that belongs to our neighbor.

That kind of coveting can create false idols in our lives and keep us distracted from God's purposes, not to mention separate us from friends and neighbors. God had a reason to squelch that kind of coveting in our lives.

As I continued to study the Bible I discovered the word "covet" in the apostle Paul's discourse on spiritual gifts: *"But covet earnestly the best gifts..."* (1 Corinthians 12:31 KJV). Throughout the years I read it many, many times, but I didn't truly understand its instruction until I was in full-time ministry in my adult years. Paul was giving an instruction on how to have spiritual gifts operate in our lives. We must earnestly, strongly desire them, particularly the ones needed for specific needs at any given moment.

> *So you should earnestly desire the most helpful gifts. But now let me show you a way of life that is best of all* (1 Corinthians 12:31 NLT).

Strongly desiring the gifts is much more than entertaining a giddy thought such as, *Oooh, I'd really like to heal the sick and cast out devils!* Thinking about the gifts is one thing, coveting them is yet another.

Coveting has to do with going after God in prayer, fasting, and specifically asking God to bring more revelation and faith for operating in the gifts. We covet or passionately desire spiritual gifts in the same way we long for and pursue the baptism of the Holy Spirit.

I want to be careful to say that this is not an issue of expecting to wait a long time for them, waiting until God thinks we are spiritually mature enough. Nor is it a matter of earning the gifts as a kind of holiness badge. Coveting is about earnestly desiring God's agenda for our lives. Coveting involves longing and searching for all the treasures the Spirit wants to share with us.

I have found as I spend significant time with Him, He makes it a point to take me into His inner storeroom where the treasures lie. He loves to take out His precious treasures and show them to me. He has shown me some, but I know there are so many more for me to see!

Everyone's walk with the Holy Spirit is unique. For me, He has revealed the gifts one at a time and on His own timetable. Some gifts came immediately after my asking for them; others I have waited awhile to see them manifest in my meetings.

I remember when I first started to covet the gifts, with extended times of prayer and fasting. My very next mission trip was to Eastern Europe. I was ministering in a church in Tartu, Estonia, and I clearly remember calling for those who needed healing to come forward around the altar.

Because I did not speak their language, I told them I would not be giving them personal prayer or instruction, but I would simply lay my hands on their heads. I asked them to believe they received their healings at the moment my hand touched their heads.

I began to pray for one young man standing in front of me. I remember the smile on his face and the openness of his heart. After I prayed for him, I moved down the line, touching heads one by one. A few yards down the line I heard a loud eruption of praise from where the first young man stood. I knew God had done something, but I kept moving to reach the others in line.

When I was finished praying, I went directly to the pastor to ask about the screams. The pastor was so excited! He told me the first young man for whom I prayed came to church with crippled feet. In fact, the pastor had picked him up from alongside of the road while he was coming to church. The young man had never been to church in his life. He walked with a severe, slow limp and had excruciating pain in his feet because his mother had thrown him out of a moving car when he was just a baby.

The pastor told me when hands were laid on him the power of God hit him from his head down to his feet. The young man began to jump up and down and run around the front, absolutely pain free. He was laughing and crying at the same time, totally aware of the healing presence of God. So impacted was he by his miracle, he immediately asked the pastor to pray with him to receive Jesus as Savior! It was amazingly wonderful to me that God's compassion and healing power so deeply touched this young man that he was changed from a sinner into a saint!

God had very quickly answered my earnest desire to see spiritual gifts at work! In this case it was a creative miracle. I was doing cartwheels on the inside and learned an important lesson that day!

So I began to seek God more intently for a demonstration of the gifts of the Spirit. As I did, I grew more notably in the word of knowledge gift and in prophetic expression. God began to put creative miracles in my heart. He was stretching my faith to believe Him. He also dealt with me about following His lead in services, not always relying on the laying on of hands.

In one particular service in Tyler, Texas, I felt the presence of God in an overwhelming way. I called for anyone desiring a healing touch to come stand in front of me around the altar. As I was listening to the voice of the Holy Spirit, the words "creative miracles" rose in my heart, and I began to call them out.

I honestly cannot remember the specifics of all who were healed at that moment, but I remember one young girl about 9 years of age. During the general prayer, I saw her cry out loud while grabbing her ear. Her mother, weeping with joy, told me God opened her deaf ear, and not one person touched her daughter that night—only Jesus!

The one miracle to yet manifest in my life and ministry, the one for which it seemed I needed greater faith, was the miracle of blind eyes opening. I knew God could do it; I had seen it happen in Dad's and in others' services. I had seen God do amazing visible miracles in my services; but in all my years of service, it had never happened and I wanted to see it.

When we ask and do not see, it is easy to become discouraged and stop coveting the gifts. I have made this mistake in my life. I have allowed the busyness of life and ministry to distract me and create in me a more laid-back approach toward the gifts. At times my prayer about a service would be less specific with regard to the gifts and more general like, "God have Your way tonight; let Your glory be manifest; save and heal people tonight." God graciously answers those prayers; but I know that the more I ask specifically, the more I see my heart's desire for those who come to the meetings.

Part of the issue is our willingness to bear the "burden" of the people in our prayer time.

I remember one time I visited the meeting of a well-known healing evangelist in Springfield, Missouri. On that particular night, it was very difficult to get into the building because the rains were pounding down on the buildings and sidewalks in bucketsful. My friend and I parked the car and we slid into the first door we could find open.

Our entry brought us into the back of the auditorium; in the midst of the massive crowd, I remember walking through what was called the "invalid" section. All around us were people on stretchers, in wheelchairs, and living with extreme handicaps and physical challenges.

As a minister of the Gospel, I remember feeling deeply in my spirit, "Oh, dear God! What kind of burden is that to bear every night in prayer? These people are each coming for a miracle. How does one man or woman walk with that burden in a service?"

The question arose out of one experience I had in Gallup, New Mexico. Dad had been sidelined by his doctors for a three-month period due to some health challenges with his heart. In the interim, he sent me to Gallup to hold a tent meeting, the very first on my own.

Up until that time, I had been his afternoon speaker, having responsibility for the people who came during that time of day. That responsibility demanded one level of faith. But, when I went to Gallup, I was suddenly responsible for the people who came to all the services. I was praying for the messages to deliver, souls to be saved, sick to be healed, and for the expenses of the meeting to be met in the offerings.

This was a whole new level of faith for me and definitely a much heavier burden to carry—a burden I felt in my mind, body, and spirit the entire week. It demanded my being in prayer for the entire day before I ministered.

God allowed me to serve in Gallup to show me the kind of burden my dad carried every night of his tent meetings in every city he visited. He taught me how to specifically pray for him and support him in better ways. He also showed me I had growing to do in the understanding of the "weight" of the anointing—both in the prayer that increases the weight and my willingness to "carry" the weight of the burden, God working with me.

Of course, the growth gradually increased through years of experience; but I don't remember recognizing the weight of that burden again until after Dad went home to glory. One year after his death I was in Managua, Nicaragua. Our team had been there for almost a week. We had powerful services for several nights in addition to amazing meetings for women, and also pastors and leaders.

The last night of the crusade was my final night to preach there. In my room while I was praying, for more than an hour I felt such a heavy burden for souls I thought I wouldn't be able to stand. It was a significant time of intercession.

When we arrived in center city at the field, over 22,000 people had gathered. The side streets were packed with onlookers. The sound equipment was set to project to everyone in the surrounding area.

As always, the service began with greetings, worship music, and solos. I couldn't wait for the preliminaries to be over, though. God had given me a message and a mandate, and I had to deliver the burden of my heart.

Finally my turn came—and when I opened my mouth, God did the rest. There was no persuasive word used, no sideshow or spectacle. That night the power of the Holy Spirit on that field drew hungry men and women to Jesus, and the altar areas were packed with new believers.

We must know, when we covet the expression of the Spirit's gifts in our lives, we will receive the challenge to pick up the burden of intercession for the souls and health of the people. God does not force it upon us; it is something we must be willing to do.

Then, every once in a while, as we continue with our patterns of prayer, fasting, and consecration, God surprises us.

Recently I was on a scouting mission to Panama. I was going to meet a group of pastors and preach in a few of their churches. Often I go into a country where I've never been to sense the leading of the Lord for a crusade in that country.

Prior to the trip my schedule was unusually busy. Although I did spend the beginning weeks of my year with a time of consecration, the time I spent praying specifically for miracles in Panama was minimal.

Usually when I'm in smaller churches, I take time to personally lay hands on those who come to the services, but on the last service of this trip, I prayed for all at the altar with one extended prayer for healing.

I didn't spend a lot of time asking who received healings. Simply, I asked for any who could tell a marked difference in their health from the time they walked in the building, to come and give testimony to God's work.

Immediately, four people moved toward the pastor to tell of their healings. The first demonstrated how God took away excruciating pain from his wrist, moving it all around and up and down—all pain was completely gone.

It was the next two who super-encouraged me. Both had come to church with nearly blind eyes. One could see images, but nothing clearly. The other had very blurred and darkened vision. Both gave testimony to God healing their eyesight completely—the first two in my personal experience of the "blind" seeing!

This was the first mission trip of my new year and I believed God was showing me something—He wanted me to know He was hearing my prayers for an increase of creative miracles. Because both persons came with partially blind eyes and left seeing, I sensed that God was telling me, "It's just the beginning. Keep pressing in, Donna. Continue to covet earnestly the best gifts. There are more on the horizon—don't give up, for you will reap in due season."

Coveting spiritual gifts is a form of spiritual hunger—a really good thing. When we hunger after the things of God, He is pleased with us and is faithful to answer our prayers.

> *Blessed are those who hunger and thirst for righteousness,* **for they shall be filled** (Matthew 5:6).

> *He has* **filled the hungry with good things***, and the rich He has sent away empty* (Luke 1:53).

*If you then, being evil, know how to give good gifts to your children, **how much more** will your heavenly Father give the Holy Spirit to those who ask Him!* (Luke 11:13)

The truth is, God never tires of our spiritual hunger or inquisitiveness. Jesus made it so very clear:

Do not fear, little flock, for it is your Father's good pleasure to give you the kingdom (Luke 12:32).

If we are going to covet something, we are right to covet the kingdom of God, His righteousness, the Holy Spirit of God, and every gift He wants to shower upon us. That passionate pursuit of God will never disappoint; it will open the doorway to all of Heaven's glory and a lifestyle of supernatural living.

Of course, my papa spent an entire lifetime pursuing all God had to offer and the anointing for miracles. He definitely coveted the best things. Let me share a few more testimonies of the resulting miracles, several of which took place on foreign soil.

CHAPTER 13

THE COVETING KIND OF FAITH MIRACLE STORIES

as told by R. W. Schambach

NO SENSE, JUST FAITH

I'll never forget the first church building I bought. It was an old Jewish community center in New Jersey. I rented it for three months and preached in it. So many folks got saved in it that I thought I might as well just buy the building and establish a church. But there was no way to do it—I didn't even have a bank account.

One day, while we were still renting, I was studying my message. I was going to preach on Deuteronomy 11:24, which says, *"Every place on which the sole of your foot treads shall be yours...."* Oh, Lord! I knew I wasn't just preaching to those people, I was preaching to myself.

I laid hands on about 500 people that night, but I couldn't wait to close the service. After it was over, I got my Bible, went outside, and I said to some of my preacher friends, "Come with me. We're going to walk around the building and lay some footprints down. I'm going to claim this thing."

I couldn't buy it. I had never had a bank account. I had never written a check. I didn't have any sense—but I had faith.

When I told my preacher friends that I was going to walk around the building and claim it, they said, "We'll wait in the car. You go ahead and walk."

I've learned this: When you put your faith to work, sometimes you have to do it all by yourself. God said every bit of ground that the soles of your feet tread on, you shall possess it. So, I walked around the building.

The next day they put a "For Sale" sign on the lawn. I pulled it out, marched down to the realtor's office, and asked him, "Who put this on my property?" He thought I was crazy, since he knew I had been renting the place.

He said, "What do you want to offer me for that building?"

I said, "Nothing."

"Well," he said, "come back when you have money."

I said, "Now hold on here a minute. I believe in starting low."

He said, "We just had an offer of $265,000. An insurance company owns it, and I know they won't sell for less than that."

Just then the Holy Ghost said, "Offer them $75,000." Now, if He had told me to offer $1 million, I would have done it, because I didn't have a dime anyway. There's no difference between $75,000 and $1 million if you don't have anything at all. Zero is zero. That's why it's always good to obey God. You don't have to be afraid of anything. You started with nothing; you're going to end with nothing.

I said, "I'll give you $75,000."

He didn't want to do it, but when I insisted, he picked up the phone and called the chairman of the board of the insurance company. Turning away from me, I could hear him say, "I have a crazy preacher in my office. I told him you folks turned down an offer of $265,000, but he told me to offer you $75,000. I told him there's no way you'll do it. And…what did you say? Would you say that one more time? Well, all right. It's your building. Yes, sir."

He hung up the phone and turned around to me. "He told me to sell it to you for $75,000."

I said, "What happened?"

Dumbfounded, the realtor explained, "The board of directors were meeting when I called. They had such a great year in life insurance that they said to give it to the preacher for $75,000, and they would take a loss on the taxes. You're not so dumb after all, are you, preacher?"

I said, "No, sir."

He said, "Now, how much money do you have for a down payment?"

I said, "Nothing."

He asked for $35,000 down. God provided $25,000. But the night before I had to come up with the money, we were still $10,000 short, and I didn't know what we'd do. A local preacher asked me, "What are you going to do?"

I said, "Nothing. I didn't do anything when I first started; I'm not going to do anything now. There's no time to worry now. There's no way God's going to let the devil whip Him in a business deal. God's the best businessman I've ever seen. He always finishes what He starts."

I sat in the office the next day and waited until ten minutes before noon. Noon was the deadline! Then a woman came walking up. I ran out to her and said, "Give it to me! Give it to me!"

She said, "How do you know I have something for you?"

I said, "I'll talk to you later; just turn it loose and give it to me. It's got to be you. God's never cut it so close!" She reached into her purse and took out a $10,000 cashier's check. I grabbed that thing and went down to the bank. The building belonged to me!

After it was over, one of those preachers who wouldn't march around the building with me in the first place called me on the phone from Englewood and said, "I found a building here in Englewood that I want for a church. Come on over and walk around it for me."

I said, "Well, I'm about twenty-eight minutes from you, but I'll make it in twenty. Wait for me. But remember, brother, if I use my feet, it's going to be my building!"

He never even bothered to hang up—just left the phone dangling and ran over to that building. He didn't just march around it; he raced around it and laid down his size ten tracks. And guess what? God gave him his building!

God has a specific inheritance for you! Learn how to trust Him, and He'll lead you right to it!

I didn't have a lick of sense. I just had faith. And God brought me through. I do have one regret, though—I wish I would have walked around the whole block!

INDIA

When I pastored a church in the early 1950s, we sponsored a missionary in India by paying his salary. He spent thirty years there—thirty long years.

On one occasion, he told me something that discouraged me from even supporting him. He said he had spent thirty years in India and had never seen one Mohammedan born again. I said, "What kind of investment am I making? We are investing money and keeping that man in India to preach the Gospel and not one soul has been saved. It is time to rearrange our priorities." So I went to India to find out what was going on.

The first time I visited in 1956, I preached to 50,000 people. I visited all the market places. I saw beggars, blind folks, and people who couldn't walk. I have never seen so many sick people. India is one of the poorest nations in the world with so many homeless, penniless people.

We invested thousands of dollars to build a structure that protected people from the hot sun so that they could hear the Gospel. On that opening day, I was so thrilled. I preached for two hours, and my interpreter translated for two hours—for a total of four hours. They wanted me to go on. When I gave the altar call, I was so disappointed. I had preached to 50,000 people, and not one soul had come to accept Jesus.

My mind went back to the missionary and I said, "Oh, Lord." But I knew God called us to do more than just preach the Word. He called us to demonstrate the Gospel.

Although no one came forward to accept Christ, and the crowd was obviously ready for the benediction, I said, "I am not done now. God says that signs follow His Word. I did what God called me to do; now I am going to let God do what He said He was going to do."

I invited three people from the audience to come forward— they were beggars. I knew who they were. One was blind, one was deaf and dumb, and the other was a crippled woman who had never walked upright. She walked in a horizontal position on the heels of her feet and the heels of her hands. She had a disease that hindered her from standing upright.

With 50,000 people watching, I laid hands on the blind woman first. I said, "In the name of Jesus, I command these blind eyes to see." Instantly, God opened her eyes and she ran through the audience, shouting in her own tongue, "I can see! I can see!"

Next I went to the deaf mute and put my fingers in his ears and my thumb on his tongue. I said, "In the name of Jesus, I command this deaf and dumb spirit to come out!" Instantly, the spirit responded and the man started speaking English within a few minutes. He didn't know his own language. He had been a deaf mute, but God had opened his ears and loosened his tongue.

When it came time to pray for the crippled woman, I said, "Now I am going to lay hands on this woman in the name of Mohammed. I am going to give him equal time." My interpreter did not want to translate this statement. "Please do what I ask you to do Sir—trust the leading of the Spirit on this." Which is more in keeping with his telling of the story in latter years. It was originally "Do what I tell you to do. You are my interpreter; I am the man of God."

Not one person in the audience expected her to get up, because they knew Mohammed was dead. I said, "Now, that is the difference between the god you serve and the God I serve. I didn't come here to put your god down; I came to lift mine up. You visit your shrine. I visit mine, but mine is empty because He is no longer there. That is the difference between the tombs. I came to let you know my Jesus is not dead—He is alive, and He is the same today as He was yesterday."

I laid hands on the woman in the name of Mohammed and said, "Rise and walk in the name of Mohammed." Someone asked me what I would have done if she had gotten up. I guess I would have converted. But she didn't get up.

So I said, "I am going to use the name that is above every name, the name of *Jesus*—the Lamb who was slain for the world. Jesus died for the people of India and for the whole world." The woman had not taken an upright step in fifty-eight years. I laid hands on her in the name of Jesus of Nazareth and said, "In the name of Jesus, rise and walk." She stood upright and walked for the first time in her life, because Jesus Christ is God!

Do you know what happened? The people in that crowd started jumping out of trees, and a mob came running toward me. I jumped behind my interpreter. I thought they were going to tar and feather me and run me out of their country. I never saw such an onslaught of people. They were yelling something at the top of their voices. I asked my interpreter, "What are they saying?"

He said, "They are hollering, 'Jesus is alive! Jesus is the Christ! Jesus is God!' They are coming to get saved." What a thrill! Not one of them came when I preached, but when they saw the demonstration of the Gospel, they came.

God has called the Church to demonstrate His power. Aren't you glad He is alive today?

> *Then Philip went down to the city of Samaria and preached Christ to them. And the multitudes with one accord heeded the things spoken by Philip, hearing and seeing the miracles which he did* (Acts 8:5-6).

HAITI

Haiti is one of the poorest nations in our hemisphere. The first time I flew to Haiti, I was met by a group of preachers. Instead of greeting me with "Welcome to Haiti," they looked at me and said, "You're not taking an offering here!"

I said, "When is the next plane out of here? You men didn't call for me. The Holy Ghost sent me down here. I'm going to take an offering, because the Bible instructs us to teach our people to give."

"But our people have no money! We're pastors. We don't even receive an offering."

I said, "Then I hold you gentlemen responsible for the poverty of your nation. If I can't make this Bible work in Haiti, I'll burn the thing. Either it's the truth or it's a lie; either it's God's book or it's man's book. I believe it's God's book."

I began to preach to the people and receive an offering from them. Those poor people opened their hearts in a wonderful way and gave about $15,000. At that time, that was unheard of in the history of Haiti. I told those pastors, "Your people need to learn the Gospel here in Haiti like people know it in Atlanta and New York City! If people can make it work there, they can make it work here!"

I told them the story of a widow woman who attended my church in inner-city Brooklyn, Mother Valez. She taught me this lesson. During a service she came to me and said, "God told me to give my rent money in the offering."

I asked her, "Mother, when is your rent due?"

"In three days," she said.

I didn't want to take her rent money. No way! I was her pastor, and I didn't want to see her in financial difficulty. I rolled that money back into her hand and told her to pay the rent.

I'll never forget what she said to me.

Are you trying to cheat me out of my blessing? You didn't ask for it, God did! Now take it!"

She hit me where it hurt. So I took her offering, humbled by her response. That woman taught me something.

Later on that week Mother Valez came to church with another offering. Not only did God pay the rent, but she had even more to give back to Him.

That wasn't the best part of her testimony, though. She and I had been praying for her sons to be saved. She said, "Brother Schambach, those two boys you and I have been praying and fasting for got saved this morning!"

This story blesses me so much because it illustrates the point that God blesses those who give, even when they are facing financial difficulty. I told this story to the people in Haiti.

The next night a Haitian woman came to me with $100. About 70,000 people were there for that service, and I wanted all of them to hear what this little lady had to say.

She said, "Remember that story Pastor told last night about that woman in Brooklyn? If God can do it in Brooklyn, He can do it here in Haiti. My rent is $160, and it's due tomorrow. I only have $100. So I'm just going to give it to God. They won't take it anyway. I'm going to trust God to do it!"

I thought, *Oh, Lord.*

And all the Haitian preachers on the platform were sitting there saying, "Oh, Lord. This ain't New York. This is Port-au-Prince."

All of a sudden I saw a man coming forward from the middle of the crowd. He said, "God spoke to me. He told me to pay that woman's rent for three months. Here's the check for it."

Another time in Haiti, I conducted a revival crusade in a stadium in Port-au-Prince. On opening night, there were 35,000 people in the stadium. That night, I prayed a prayer for the people and left.

On my way out, a 12-year-old boy wrapped his hands around my leg and would not turn loose. While I was dragging him, he was saying something in Creole. I couldn't understand him, so I asked, "What in the world is he saying?"

My driver said, "I'll interpret for you. This boy is telling you he was born blind. When you prayed that one prayer, the lights came on. He can see!"

I picked up the boy and put him in the arms of one of the preachers and said, "Take him up there and let him tell the story." When we were driving out, it sounded like somebody had made a touchdown in there! The people had heard the boy's testimony.

Now, everybody in Port-au-Prince knew that boy. He had begged on the streets, and everyone knew he was totally blind. The news of his miracle spread, and the next night the stadium was jam-packed with about 70,000 people, with many more outside who couldn't get in.

That triggered many more miracles throughout the entire crusade.

INDONESIA

I want to share with you some amazing stories that took place in Indonesia. But first I want to say a little bit about the baptism of the Holy Ghost.

I'm not ashamed to preach about the baptism of the Holy Ghost. A lot of preachers don't believe in this, or they are ashamed to speak it from the pulpit. Not me! I like to shout it from the rooftops. I like to splash it all over television and radio. I like to let people know that God wants to fill them with the Holy Ghost and fire!

Read with me in Acts 2:1-4:

> *When the Day of Pentecost had fully come, they were all with one accord in one place. And suddenly there came a sound from heaven, as of a rushing mighty wind, and it filled the whole house where they were sitting. Then there appeared to them divided tongues, as of fire, and one sat upon each of them. And they were all filled with the Holy Spirit and began to speak with other tongues, as the Spirit gave them utterance.*

The record is very clear that the tongues of fire sat upon each of them, and they were all filled with the Holy Ghost. And when they were all filled with the Holy Ghost, they began to speak in tongues as the Spirit gave them utterance. Before the day of Pentecost, there is no record that any person ever spoke an unlearned language as a result of the moving of God's Spirit.

In Acts 2, it talks of a *"rushing mighty wind," "tongues, as of fire,"* and says that they were speaking *"with other tongues."* Later in Acts 10, it says they were speaking with tongues and magnifying God. And in Acts 19, it refers to speaking with tongues and prophecy.

In each instance, there was an additional manifestation, but only speaking with tongues occurred every time. You see, this was to be the initial evidence that believers had been filled with the Holy Ghost. It signified that the early church had received *"the promise of the Father"* and *"the Comforter"* whom Jesus had promised.

Well, the Holy Ghost is just as real to us in this day as He was for the early church. I have experienced this many times, but one of the greatest examples I have seen came when I was preaching in Indonesia. About 30,000 people gathered on a field to hear me preach.

That day I was tired. I had been preaching all through the area. I had preached to so many people, and I was really tired in my body. When I was getting ready to preach that day, I prayed, "Oh, Lord. Please spare this old flesh of mine. Let Your Spirit come on everybody who's out in that field."

All of a sudden, 10,000 people fell down under the power of God. Like a breath of wind! I looked in front of me, and 10,000 more people fell. Then I looked to the side, and the last 10,000 people fell. Right there in front of me! No catchers. They were all fallers, and they all fell down right on the field.

There I was, standing all by myself. So I looked around at my interpreter, and he was out! I said, "Lord, I feel like I've been left out. Knock me out, too."

God said, "Walk through the crowd of the people."

So I walked out there. Toward the back, there was group of young people, Indonesian young people. They were speaking in English. In English! It blew my mind.

I ran up and got my interpreter off the ground and said, "Get up, quick!"

"What?" he replied. "What do you want me to do?"

I said, "Come with me. I want you to see and hear what I found."

So he came back with me and I showed him.

"You got me up out of the Spirit for this?" he said. "Oh, Brother Schambach, that's a common occurrence. They're receiving the Holy Ghost. They don't know English, but this is a sign to them that they received the baptism of the Holy Ghost."

You see, I know English. It's not an unknown tongue to me. It wasn't to my interpreter either. He knew English as well as his native language. But these young people didn't know English. Nobody had ever taught them. It was the utterance of the Holy Spirit. That was the initial evidence to them.

You might be wondering about the baptism of the Holy Ghost. Your pastor might tell you that it's not for today, or that it's not for everyone today, just some. Well, I'm telling you it's for you.

God has provided a mighty in-filling of the Holy Ghost and power to carry His people over the turbulent times of these last days. You need this! It is for you! Let God baptize you in the Holy Ghost and fire!

There was another miracle that took place in Indonesia that blew my mind. I cannot explain how it happened. All I know is that it happened.

I was conducting meetings in Semarang. On the opening night, there was torrential downpour. I mean, everything was drenched. (I really know when to have an outdoor meeting!) But the place was still packed. Not one of those people moved. They stood there and listened to me preach.

Some of my associates wanted to give me an umbrella to put over me, but I said, "No. If they're going to stand in the rain to hear me, I'm going to preach to them in the rain."

So I preached to them in the rain! And God did so many great miracles that day. I laid hands on people. Blind eyes were opened. Deaf ears were opened. Cripples were walking. It was powerful!

Because of the large crowd, there were army guards all around. They'd never had crowds of that capacity before. One of these soldiers, who was a colonel in the army and a Muslim, came to me and asked, "Would you pray for me?"

"What's wrong with you?" I said.

"Well, I got shot in this eye. The bullet is still in there, and I can't see out of that eye."

Now, I knew this man was a Muslim. So I made it clear to him what name I pray in—the name of Jesus. He is the only miracle-worker. Mohammed can't hear me pray because he is still in the grave. But Jesus is alive! Hallelujah!

"I pray in the name of Jesus," I told him.

"Use any name you want," he replied. "I've seen too much here!"

So I prayed for that colonel in the name of Jesus. I can't explain what happened after that. It is hard to fathom! I am not a chemist. I'm not a scientist. But after I put my hand on that eye and asked God to perform a miracle, the bullet melted right into my hand, and God restored perfect vision to the eye.

That man got saved and filled with the Spirit, and God called him to preach.

Now, he would have been up for retirement in six months, but he went immediately and resigned his commission! He said, "I want to travel all over Indonesia and tell my people that Jesus is Lord!"

Listen to me. He wasn't saved when God performed the miracle. He was still a sinner. Many Christians don't like to hear that. But God did it anyway, and it was that miracle that opened his eyes to the Gospel, and to the power of Jesus Christ. Then God used him to shake up Indonesia!

There was another Muslim man who came to me for a miracle in Suribia, Indonesia. But this one was not a soldier. He was a priest. He brought his wife to me—she was demon-possessed. Doctors couldn't help her. His religion couldn't help her. She was bound by the devil.

So he brought her to me for prayer. Then when I laid hands on her, the strangest thing happened. All of a sudden, there were thumbtacks and nails coming out of her skin. I've never seen anything like it before. God delivered her and set her free.

The next night the man came back to the service. While I was receiving the offering, he came up to the front and threw something in the bucket. It was wrapped up in a newspaper, and was so heavy that the bucket fell out of my hand.

I grabbed him by the shoulder and pulled him back. I said, "What in the world do you have in there?"

"Look," he said.

I opened it up and discovered that it was a brick of solid gold!

Then he told his story: "I've had my wife everywhere. Doctors couldn't do anything. My religion couldn't do anything. I brought her here and you laid hands on her in the name of Jesus, and she was delivered. I answered that altar call, and now I'm a Jesus man. And I wanted to bring you that offering."

I gave the gold to our missionary there and told him to build a new home for orphans.

AFRICA

In Africa, in a church with a crowd of 6,000 people, I suddenly stopped preaching. In the back there was a man sitting in the aisle, talking with his hands. I knew he was interpreting for the deaf. The anointing of God came on me. I stopped and said, "Brother, you back there in that aisle, you are disturbing me." He wasn't saying anything vocally, but he was conveying my message to people who couldn't hear. I wanted to capture his attention. And you know I did when I said that. I continued, "Brother, I am getting tired of you talking while I am talking. Bring all those deaf folks up here. God is going to heal them now."

Seventeen of them got up—seventeen deaf mutes in Africa. I lined them up on the platform facing the people. The cameras were on. We were on television. The pastor of the church was nervously sitting on the edge of his chair.

I looked at the deaf people and saw one boy smiling from ear to ear.

"Yeah," I said to myself, "he's expecting something."

I had been preaching that Jesus Christ is the same today as He was yesterday. Well, if you believe that, demonstrate it. Paul said:

> *And I, brethren, when I came to you, did not come with excellence of speech or of wisdom declaring to you the testimony of God. ...And my speech and my preaching were not with persuasive words of human wisdom, but in demonstration of the Spirit and of power, that your faith should not be in the wisdom of men but in the power of God* (1 Corinthians 2:1,4-5).

I believe in what I preach. So I began to talk to the boy. I don't know sign language, so the man started to interpret. I said to the man, "I don't need you anymore. Go sit down."

I put my finger in the boy's ears and in the name of Jesus took authority over that deaf and dumb spirit. I felt the spirit slide right by my finger. I knew he had come out—I knew it! I knew the boy's ears had opened. I spent about ten minutes with the lad and started teaching him English.

The pastor of the church was so blessed, he did a somersault in midair—and he was not an acrobat!

I went down the line. I got hold of a woman, cast the spirit out of her, and taught her to speak. I said to the pastor, "Bring the rest of your pastors here." There were thirty-five of them. I said, "Line them up. I'm not going to wear myself out. Let them wear themselves out. Tell them to put their fingers in the people's ears. Tell them to put a thumb on their tongues. I will pray one prayer, and God will heal all fifteen of them."

I prayed one prayer, talked to the deaf and dumb spirit, and in the name of Jesus commanded it to come out. The pastor took the microphone on television and went down the line. Each one heard and spoke.

CHAPTER 14

KEY #7: SPIRITUAL PERCEPTION

Donna Schambach

We were in Brno in the Czech Republic, invited by a signifi-cant church to do an evangelistic crusade in a rather large hockey rink in the city. Quite a lot of advertisement had gone out in Brno, and on opening night the seating areas and floor of the arena were just about filled to capacity.

As the worship service began, I realized only the first few rows of people were actually entering into worship. Most were sitting and watching with arms folded and stern expressions on their faces. We certainly didn't feel the warm welcome we usually received when walking into a church.

These folks were either from a Russian Orthodox background or just plain heathens. No "great waves of faith" arose from the seating area. We had a house filled with spectators.

155

In the beginning, the service was rather tame, progressing nicely. Then our hosts introduced Dad as the evening speaker. I remember he preached a masterpiece of a message on faith, building a solid theological platform for believing in Christ Jesus. He was crystal clear about the work of Christ on the cross and the need to embrace His salvation by faith.

Usually after a message like that, he would immediately head into his altar call. He loved to see people get saved! But this night was different. He had spotted a young man who was deaf and mute before the service, and he asked for those who knew him to bring him to the front of the auditorium.

The young man looked puzzled and a little frightened, so Dad tried to communicate with sign language that he wanted to pray for the youth's ears to be opened.

All eyes were on Dad and this boy as Dad put his fingers in his ears and commanded the deaf spirits to leave. Then Dad took his first finger out of the left ear and loudly spoke into it, "OPEN!"

The boy was so surprised that he didn't know whether to laugh or cry. His eyes were staring in wonder. Then Dad went to the right ear: "OPEN!" he commanded the right ear, and that ear opened too!

By now the young boy was holding both ears and smiling. Dad turned him around toward the audience and asked them to clap their hands. When they did, the smile on the young man's face got broader and broader.

And then Dad began to teach him how to say his first words. He had the young man speaking the name of Jesus and counting in English almost immediately.

After that healing was accomplished and verified several times, Dad talked about the living Jesus—His power to heal deaf ears and free a life from sin. Then he invited those who wanted to receive Jesus as Savior to come forward. To my astonishment, more than half of the audience, most of them starting the service with stern looks, rose to come to the front and surrender to Jesus.

THE EYE OF THE SPIRIT

The next day I quizzed Dad when we were alone. I had been watching him from the platform. Before he called that boy, I saw him looking and watching as though he were looking for something. I recognized that look—it is not a look that comes from the natural eye—he was looking with the eye of the Spirit. He was searching out what the Father was already doing.

> So Jesus explained, "I tell you the truth, the Son can do nothing by himself. He does **only what he sees the Father doing.** Whatever the Father does, the Son also does" (John 5:19 NLT).

I knew why Dad brought that boy up to the front of the auditorium. I understood well the miracle would point to the power of the Living Christ. That was perfectly logical. But I had to ask, "How in the world did you know that boy would be healed?"

In my mind I was thinking Dad took a huge risk. He was in a foreign country with a large group of unbelievers. They were not going to go easy on him. That could have been the end of the crusade. (My analytical mind was working overtime.)

Dad answered the question, but he didn't give me a long, drawn-out theological explanation. He simply said, "I just knew."

I partially understood what he meant. He was operating by the Spirit of God, and at that point in time he was in the spiritual realm. "God was working with him," as the Scriptures explain. I was witnessing an integral part of Dad's evangelistic ministry.

> *How God anointed Jesus of Nazareth with the Holy Spirit and with power, who went about doing good and healing all who were oppressed by the devil, for* **God was with Him** *(Acts 10:38).*

> *Now when they had come and gathered the church together, they reported* **all that God had done with them***, and that He had opened the door of faith to the Gentiles* (Acts 14:27).

I wouldn't fully understand what Dad meant until God began to work with me in my services through the gifts of the Holy Spirit.

As explained in Chapters 6 and 7 focusing on compassion, God moves the heart of the minister toward the need that God wants to meet. *Spiritual perception,* on the other hand, is our ability to see what God is doing and hear what He is saying, this gives us greater accuracy with the word of knowledge, the gifts of healing, and the working of miracles.

The best way I can explain this in the natural is to say that it is as though the minister becomes "cocooned" in an airtight bubble of the anointing. At that time, we are ministering on another frequency, tuned in to Heaven, following orders in the midst of "The Cloud."

At times, the Holy Spirit may draw me to specific people; I might see light or a glow around certain people; I might get a word picture while I'm praying for someone; or I may feel directed to pray a specific Bible verse over another. It is all about seeing and hearing on a different plane.

VOCALIZATION OF FAITH

Spiritual perception and working the supernatural have several components. In addition to the heart of compassion and the eye of the Spirit, there is another very important element—*the vocalization of faith*.

When we "see" or "picture" what God wants to do in a life, we begin to speak it out. This is so important because it is the exercise of our spiritual authority. This is part of "speaking to the mountain," about which Jesus spoke:

> *So Jesus answered and said to them, "Have faith in God. For assuredly, I say to you, whoever says to this mountain, 'Be removed and be cast into the sea,' and does not doubt in his heart, but believes that those things he says will be done, he will have whatever he says. Therefore I say to you, whatever things you ask when you pray, believe that you receive them, and you will have them"* (Mark 11:22-24).

I remember sincerely praying to be used in the word of knowledge and in the prophetic. At that time God was putting word pictures and scenarios in my mind's eye with regard to specific people. I was seeing things like a cluster of grapes and a kernel of corn.

I did not receive the full revelation about those things at the same time I saw the pictures in my heart; but later in the services, as I dared to *speak out* what I had seen earlier, the simple pictures developed into detailed prophetic words, fluently pouring out of my spirit. They had accurate relevance to the persons involved—things I could have never known in the natural.

There is a "flow" to our spiritual perception and moving in the power of the Spirit:

- Compassion, leads us toward the need.
- The eye of the Spirit reveals the specifics of the need.
- The voice of authority calls the miracle into action.

Of all three steps, the last has been the most challenging for me. Because I never wanted to be wrong or embarrassed, it took me awhile to get comfortable with the *vocalizing* part.

In one specific service in my home state of Texas, God had shown me five distinct scenarios while I was praying in my hotel room. I saw one woman unpacking a suitcase. Another gentleman was climbing into a truck to go on a long journey. There were other pictures that I cannot recall today; but there was one picture that came to me, I shall never forget. I saved that one for last in the service, because I didn't want to speak it out.

We were in the middle of the worship service and the glory of the Lord was strong. I had never been to this church previously, but the pastor had made me feel very welcomed.

A LISTENING EAR

In an unusual manner for me, during the worship service I stood up with a boldness and authority. The pastor, who was standing in front of me to my left, without batting an eye, stretched out the microphone for me to grab it from his right hand. There was no exchange of words, just a passing of the microphone. The Holy Spirit was orchestrating the service.

At once, all five people about whom God had given me specific word pictures, lit up as though they had halos on their heads. I didn't know their names, so I pointed to them and called them to stand in the front. One by one I began to speak the word pictures out to them, and each one began to break, weep, and worship the Lord. God was doing a strong and a deep work that day.

I finished delivering four messages, and the fifth one was waiting patiently. He was an older man, standing round-shouldered and expressionless. He didn't look like he was "into" the service at all; I was very hesitant to share the word picture God gave me for him.

Publically I said, "The last picture I have in my heart is for this man. I cannot explain why the Lord showed me this picture, and I hesitate to share it. I only share it in obedience."

"Sir," I began cautiously, "I see you dressed in grave clothes." As soon as the words left my mouth, the entire congregation gasped in unison. I had no idea why.

"The grave clothes are like mummies' cloths wrapped around your head and shoulders. There is a death grip on your mind and emotions. You are encumbered with a spirit of oppression, trying to kill you. It is as though the spirit of death is stalking you."

The whole time I was speaking I was aware of the congregation gasping and whispering and the pastor brushing away tears from his face. They knew something I didn't know.

I began to pray for him with the Holy Spirit's help, and he began to weep and crumble under the weight of God's presence. His shoulders kept folding in, time and time again, as if His heart was being broken and put back together again. I remember him falling on his knees before God with uncontrollable sobs as those in the church gathered around him to pray with him.

The service ended and I was escorted to the back for a time of refreshment. A little later the pastor joined me and one of the first

161

questions he asked me was, "Do you know the story of the last man you prayed for?"

"No, sir, "I asserted, "I never saw the man before tonight. I don't even know his name."

"Well, that's what I thought. You couldn't have; but the Holy Spirit knew. About two months ago, not long before Christmas, he walked in on his only daughter, who at the time had a gun to her head. When he moved closer to stop her, he saw his daughter pull the trigger and kill herself."

Now it was my turn to gasp.

"We have had to watch him closely. He has been to a psychiatrist and the doctor has worried about him committing suicide too. The guilt of how he treated his daughter at times, the image of her killing herself, and the agony of such a loss at her young age have all been too much for him. He has been walking around in a cloud of dark oppression.

"But tonight, God has done something for him. God has set him free," I said.

I received a letter from the pastor about two months later. He wrote to tell me the same man God delivered died in his sleep. He was with Jesus now. Had he died before that service, no one knew where he might spend eternity. After the service in which God let me see what He was seeing; after the man's heart was clean before the Father, we all knew the man was now home in the presence of Jesus.

When we recognize the Holy Spirit's signs and begin to "see" what others around us miss, we gain a boldness that may be unusual for us to manifest naturally. The more we tune in to that channel, the more people around us will be touched and blessed.

A SEEING EYE

Years ago I traveled with my father and a rather large team to a significant church in Europe. Our trip had been long and exhausting, with several stops along the way for meetings. By the time we arrived at the host-church city, I was nearly delirious in my physical body from lack of sleep and was ready for a long nap.

I wasn't able to rest right away because one of the pastors from the host church was coming to the hotel to have dinner with Dad and the team. This was not the lead pastor, but someone I had met once or twice before on my ministry trips.

The conversation around the table was jovial and pleasant. Mostly we talked about families and ministry, keeping the discussion light. No important issues were discussed that day. Our host knew we were ready for rest and he excused us promptly.

What happened next was a mystery to me for a number of years. I went to my room to lie down on the bed, and the thought flashed across my spirit with a stereo boom, "He will be leaving to start a church in another city."

Well, I didn't know the pastor well, but I knew him well enough to know he was a loyal man to the lead pastor. He didn't do things rashly and he was really vested in that significant church he helped to establish in Europe.

The Lord began to show me his leaving would be of the Holy Spirit, and when the time came to leave, his pastor would know it was God and send him off with his blessing. Then the Lord instructed me to write down all of these impressions in a note and give it to the pastor I hardly knew.

Oh how I struggled, not with writing the note, but with the decision to give it to him. I knew I had severe jet lag and was almost delirious in my physical body. Furthermore, I didn't know him or his relationship with the church beyond a casual acquaintance. And, I was a single woman giving a married man a note—how would that look? The man would think I was crazy at best, improper at worst.

But I felt strongly I had heard from God. So I wrote the note, took a very long nap, and the next day I handed it to him. (To cover the single woman thing, I included an offering for him to take his wife out to dinner.)

Well, that entire trip he never answered me. In fact, he didn't talk to me much the rest of our time there, except to thank me for the offering. As we were leaving, I overheard him say to Dad, "I am very happy here." Which, of course, I interpreted as, "You got this one wrong, Donna."

Years later, I was ministering in Eastern Europe and this same pastor was also there to minister. After the services I was invited to have dinner with all the guest ministers. While at the table, this pastor began a very interesting conversation, "Sister Donna, I don't know if you remember several years ago handing me a note."

"Yes, I do brother."

"Well, at first I thought it was absolutely wrong—had nothing to do with me, but I kept it and placed it in a drawer. Several years later our lead pastor began to challenge us to win more souls to Jesus, particularly those we know. I began to have a burden for my hometown. It was very strong and almost overwhelming. The Lord began to put into my spirit to start a church there."

He continued the intriguing story: "I was almost afraid to approach our lead pastor as we had done ministry together forever. But I knew God was speaking to me. Before I went in to speak with him, I rediscovered your note and I took it with me to show him. He listened to me talk about the burden of my heart intently, and when I showed him the note he said, 'This is God!'

"Sister Donna," he concluded, "God used you to confirm a new work he wanted me to do. I wanted you to know that."

I was very happy he shared that story with me; I had been feeling as though I hadn't heard the voice of the Holy Spirit properly. Instead, it was just an issue of timing.

The truth is, we may never know how accurate we are when delivering a word from the Lord to someone. We simply must continually yield ourselves, as vessels of clay, to His leading. Sometimes we may miss it. Other times it will be exactly the right word for a future time. Our job is to cultivate a *listening ear* and a *seeing eye*.

Let's return now to Dad's inspirational stories and see how he learned to partner with God's supernatural power—because you can, too!

CHAPTER 15

MIRACLE STORIES OF HOLY SPIRIT DIRECTION

by R. W. Schambach

"I DIED LAST NIGHT"

I'll never forget one of the most unusual things that happened under the tent. It was during one of the greatest revivals I have ever had—and a man died in the fourth row.

Immediately I went to him with my Bible. I wasn't going to let the devil kill anybody in my meeting. I commanded the devil to turn him loose. I called his spirit back into his body. There were no signs of life. I told my tent crew, "Come and take him behind the platform. No one is going to disturb my preaching." They took him there. Somehow we actually forgot about him.

The next night I returned to the tent. During the meeting I asked, "I want five of the happiest people here tonight to come up and tell us what you are happy about."

The dead man was first in line!

I didn't recognize him. He was dressed up. I handed him the microphone and asked, "What are you happy about, brother?"

"Praise God!" he replied. "I died last night."

I thought, *What kind of nut do I have here?*

But he looked at me in a strange way and said, "Don't you remember me?"

"No sir," I replied. "I don't remember you."

"You walked through four rows of chairs to get to me," he answered. "Brother Schambach, I had my fifth heart attack in your tent last night. Doctors told me if I had one more heart attack, it would kill me. My body was there, but my spirit was gone. I saw you running back through those people. You called my spirit back into my body."

Tears started running down his face. "I am so thankful you did that," he said, "because last night I was a sinner and I would have gone to hell if you hadn't stopped my spirit. My spirit came back into my body. I woke up behind that platform with a brand-new heart. I got saved and filled with the Holy Ghost last night. I went to my doctor today, and he couldn't believe it."

The man shouted, "Jesus came into my heart last night and gave me a brand-new heart. Hallelujah!"

His doctor had said to him, "Where are the other four scars on your heart?" He couldn't find the scars from the previous attacks. "You have the heart of a 25-year-old man."

Since that night, when God directs me, I don't hesitate to lay hands on any dead folks because they may not be saved. I would like them to be saved—saved from the burning flames of hell! That man was on his way to hell; but thank God, I got hold of that spirit before the devil could claim him. God saved him and filled him with the Holy Ghost and with fire.

THE FIRST DEVIL I EVER CAST OUT

I will never forget the first devil I cast out. I was with Brother A. A. Allen in Los Angeles. He cast the devils out of a girl who came to our meeting. We then moved to Phoenix, and when I saw her walk inside the tent, I said, "Oh, Lord, they are all back, plus another thousand."

When Brother Allen saw her, he said, "Do you see what I see?"

I said, "Yes, sir."

"Oh," he said, "I can't tackle them tonight. If I pray for the sick, I won't be able to deliver her also. Take her in the prayer tent and cast them out."

I said, "What? You are the preacher."

He said, "I won't have anybody working with me who doesn't know how to cast out devils."

This was "where the rubber met the road." This was the "nitty gritty" now. This wasn't just playing church. I went to the platform and asked twelve of the pastors to come with me.

They said, "Where are we going?"

I said, "To battle. We are going to the prayer tent to battle." I picked six women with husky voices. I said, "Get the Blood songs ready. Just sing Blood songs. We are going to conquer the devil."

I was there from ten o'clock at night until one o'clock in the morning wrestling with those demons. I wrestled with the devils. It felt as though I had lost thirty pounds casting out those demons.

For we do not wrestle against flesh and blood, but against principalities, against powers, against the rulers of the darkness of this age, against spiritual hosts of wickedness in the heavenly places (Ephesians 6:12).

I said, "Devil, in the name of Jesus, you are coming out."

The devil answered me, "We are not coming out."

It wasn't just, "I am not" but, *"We* are not."

I wanted to say, "Go ahead, fella, stay where you are. I'm not going to bother you."

But we ganged up on them. I quoted every Scripture passage I knew. I found out you can't beat the air and pound them out. You can't stomp them out. You can't knock them out. You can't Scripture-quote them out. You have to *cast* them out. This is what God told us to do. Finally, at three o'clock in the morning, the devil said, "We are going to wear you out."

He didn't know how close to the truth he was. I said, "Devil, we don't wear out." I felt like somebody put a mantle on me. I said, "Satan, my elder brother Jesus destroyed you 2,000 years ago." The moment I said, the voice inside that woman said, "Don't say that."

I said, "I got him. I got him!" So, being an obedient servant, I shouted it again. I learned my lesson a long time ago. When the devil tells you not to do something, do it. And when he tells you to do something, you don't do it.

I said, "He has his bags packed. He is on his way." I shouted it louder one more time.

The devil said, "I know it. But don't say it so loud. Everybody doesn't know it."

When Jesus died on Calvary and shed His blood, He paid the price. I believe the devils came out of everybody so they could gather around the cross of Calvary and wring their hands and say, "We got Him now."

But they didn't have Him! Jesus died on the cross, defeating sin and satan. No one destroyed the kingdom of the devil like Jesus did!

> *I am He who lives, and was dead, and behold, I am alive forevermore. Amen. And I have the keys of Hades and of Death* (Revelation 1:18).

Those devils finally came out of that woman. I made sure that she received Christ into her heart and was baptized in the Holy Ghost. When we heard her speaking in other tongues, we knew those devils would never return again. Praise God!

> *You are of God, little children, and have overcome them, because He who is in you is greater than he who is in the world* (1 John 4:4).

WALKING THE STREETS OF SOUTH PHILLY

The Bible says, *"God has not given us a spirit of fear..."* (2 Timothy 1:7). It also says, *"...fear involves torment..."* (1 John 4:18). Therefore, I can conclude that fear is a tormenting spirit. Many of God's people are bound by this tormenting spirit of fear, even when they hear the Word preached.

Fear is the opposite of faith. It can keep you from being active as a Christian. If you are bound with a spirit of fear, I don't have to tell you—you need a miracle of deliverance. And I have good news—God wants you to be rid of fear in your life and is ready and willing to set you free.

Once, when I was in Philadelphia, I met a woman who had a problem with fear.

I used to conduct private interviews where people could come and meet with me one on one. This lady came in trying to make an impression. She talked in tongues a little and then sat down.

I said, "What can I do for you?"

She said, "I've come for you to pray for me."

I said, "I don't pray in the daytime. I pray at night. You see, we preach in the daytime to stir your faith. Then we lay hands on you during the night service when faith is alive."

She said, "Well, I can't come at night."

I said, "Are you working?"

"No."

"Do you have an appointment?"

"No."

"Then come back tonight," I told her.

"I'm not coming back."

I said, "Well, I'm not praying."

That might seem harsh, but I knew she was hiding something from me. I discerned it in my own spirit. So I asked her, "What's your problem? I want to know."

She said, "Well, I've got high blood pressure, and I've got sugar diabetes."

"Is that all?" I said.

"Yes, it is," she replied.

I said, "No, you're telling me a lie. You're telling me you can't come tonight. The reason why you can't come is because you're bound with a spirit of fear."

She said, "How did you know?"

Listen, she was a child of God. She loved the Lord. But she was still bound by the spirit of fear.

She said, "I haven't been out of my house at night for the past twelve years. Oh, Brother Schambach, this spirit torments me."

I said, "Look, stay until tonight. Go next door and buy a sandwich. Stay here, and I'll pray for you tonight. I'll get rid of that spirit of fear. God's given me the power to cast out devils, and I'm going to liberate you from that foul spirit that's tormenting your mind. If you stay, and God doesn't deliver you, my wife and I will personally take you home."

She said, "You'll do that?"

I said, "I'll do it. I'll even go into your house first. You can stay with my wife in the car. I'll turn on every light, look behind the couch and the chairs, open your closet, and make sure there's nobody around there."

She was convinced. She said, "Well, if you'll do that, I'll stay."

After I preached that night, I called her up first for prayer. I laid hands on her and the power of God hit her and knocked her flat on her back. I laid hands on about 500 people that night.

After it was all over, my wife and I were looking for the woman because I'd promised to give her a ride home. But I couldn't find her anywhere! I ran outside and looked all over the place. I said, "Oh, Lord. I've got to find that woman." I never did.

The next night she came back into the meeting shouting and rejoicing. At night!

I said, "Come on up here. I know you've got a testimony."

She told the people the story I told you. She said, "I know Brother Schambach told me he and his wife would take me home last night. But I didn't have to let them take me home because when he laid hands on me, that devil of fear left. God delivered me and set me free! I walked the whole way home."

I said, "You walked? In Philadelphia?"

Now I was getting nervous! She lived thirty blocks away in South Philadelphia. That meant she had walked through the worst part of town! This was the same woman who was afraid to go out at night!

She said, "I got there at about three o'clock in the morning. I put the key in the latch, but I felt so good that I took it back out and walked the streets all night long saying, 'Devil, you're a liar. I'm not afraid of you anymore!'"

God delivered her from fear! If you are bound with a spirit of fear, He wants to do the same thing for you. You don't have to be afraid anymore. You can turn around and face the enemy with confidence because God is on your side!

Let me pray for you:

> *Father, in Jesus' name, I come to You on behalf of this reader who's bound by fear. Thank You for the authority You've given me over devils. Fear, you foul, tormenting spirit, I adjure you by Jesus—loose your hold on this person's life. I command it in the name of Jesus. Lord, give him or her a miracle of deliverance, and give him or her the strength to stand up against the enemy. In Jesus' name, I call it done. Amen and amen.*

CHAPTER 16

KEY #8: CONSECRATION AND HOLINESS

Donna Schambach

CONSECRATION

By Jesus' own example there were times He often went away by Himself to pray. Many times He went to the mountains. He also went to the wilderness to fast and pray.

The Bible doesn't give us many glimpses into Jesus' actual prayers, but we do see the results of His prayer times. When He came back from His private times with the Father, He came back filled up with spiritual strength and He was able to see exactly what the Father wanted to do. It was after these times of consecration that Jesus performed His greatest miracles.

Time for consecration is something that has often been lost on this generation. We are an instant-gratification, fast-moving society, and in many ways we have grown impatient and have forgotten how to wait on anything.

While it is true the Holy Spirit is always with us, and we can always pray and be heard—there is something about being alone for a day, several days, a week or more, if directed. Days specifically set aside for time with God can be the most restorative times for a believer. And during these times, direction from God seems clearer than ever.

My dad often spoke of the times when the Lord led him to consecrate extended fasts during specific meetings. One of those times he was in Florida. He often spoke about those meetings as being some of the most powerful, with mighty miracles taking place all week long.

During one meeting the Lord led Dad to give away his only 18-wheeler—the one he used to carry His tent equipment. It was old, but he needed it. Although it took some heavenly persuasion to have him release it, he gave it to a young preacher. The next day a trucker dropped by Dad's office in Elwood City, Pennsylvania. He told Sister Sorbo, Dad's secretary, that God instructed him to give Brother Schambach his brand-new Kenworth.

Dad was shouting over the news. Then, before the meeting in Florida ended, someone sold him five 18-wheelers for $35,000. Each one of them was a new Kenworth, considered the Cadillac of the semi world at that time. The sale of five Kenworths for $35,000 was a remarkable price in the 1970s, a true miracle of provision.

Dad also often mentioned a crusade in Indonesia. Admittedly, his fast there was a kind of forced fast for about a week because he couldn't find good food. Again, during that fast, the miracles were outstanding.

He specifically remembers a blind Muslim woman receiving her sight. Her husband had been a Muslim priest, but when he saw what Jesus did, he immediately converted and started preaching about Jesus. That man also brought a large offering the next night. When he placed it in the offering bucket, the bucket dropped out of Dad's hand. The man had brought a gold brick to thank the Lord for opening his wife's blind eyes. With that brick, Dad was able to help purchase a building for an orphanage, one we supported for many years to come.

In my own life, I usually set two or three 21-day periods aside for partial fasting and what I call consecration. During that time, I don't watch television or have other forms of entertainment. I try to limit my social media and spend my time reading, studying, and praying. I have found that those times provide sensitivity to the Spirit's voice like no other for me. When I go to my next meetings, I operate more keenly in the prophetic word and words of knowledge. Also, I see the ministry "business" flow so much better.

An important part of consecration times is meditation. One of my favorite books is Richard Foster's *Celebration of Discipline*. He is a Quaker who has given keen insight into the discipline of meditation. He teaches the difference between meditation in Eastern religions and biblical meditation. Rather than "emptying our minds" to achieve peace, biblical meditation involves "filling ourselves up" with the Word of God and reflecting on its meaning to us and our circumstance.

Meditation is like "chewing" on the Word—the Bread of Life—enjoying its flavor and receiving all of its nourishment. God has given me many, many revelations in Scripture during this meditative part of my consecration times.

Honestly, setting aside time for prayer and fasting doesn't come easy. I am single with no children and yet I still must mentally resolve to honor my commitment to consecration times, no matter what comes my way.

In the beginning stages, I failed miserably. I was tested, and I am quite sure you will be too. It seemed the moment I declared a time for consecration, everyone else wanted to party. Many different situations would arise at the same time demanding my attention. Distraction after distraction would ensue, until I gave in.

Eventually I learned how to push through the distractions. I held to my alone time and would not be sidetracked by food, parties, or fellowship. When that holy resolve began to land in my spirit, the distractions lessened.

If you are hungry for God to use you in miracles and in the supernatural, I challenge you to begin a lifestyle of consecration throughout the year. I have minister friends who have worked out their patterns with God in different ways.

Some commit to a twenty-one to forty-day fast, one or two times in a year. Others have chosen to fast the first three days of every month. Another has chosen to fast the same day each week. Think about this, if you consistently fasted one day each week, you would have fasted fifty-two days in a year—that is more than most!

Remember, we are not in some contest in which God's servants are competing for "achievement" awards. Rather, these are "pressing-in" times—times for us to experience a greater awareness of God's presence, power, and purpose. When we have a pattern that we can remain faithful to, God will consistently honor it.

HOLINESS

Another key to operating in Holy Spirit power is the very place in which we learn authority, compassion, childlikeness, and sensitivity to the Holy Spirit: the place of holiness.

We who serve the Lord are priests, representing His holiness and presence, and going before Him on behalf of others. Old Testament priests had a prescribed way to worship God, set apart from all the other Israelites. Their clothes, food choices, and every ritual they performed were mandated as a pattern of purity and wholeness.

The New Testament says we have become a kingdom of priests (Revelation 1:6) with everyone having a place of service before the Lord. That means we must be holy, for He is holy.

Holiness, as explained by the Word of God, has three expressions in time: positional holiness; actual holiness; final holiness. Let's examine each more closely.

The first is *positional holiness*. Everyone who receives Jesus as Savior can boldly walk into the presence of God, because Jesus has become our High Priest and Intercessor. His blood has washed away every sin, and we have become "the righteousness of God in Him." In Jesus, we have been made right before God; our debt of sin was paid; we have been justified, just as if we never sinned.

It is a glorious truth, my position before God is secure because I approach the Father, with Jesus standing in front of me. I cannot earn salvation or favor with God. Jesus freely gave me salvation as a gift, through His death and resurrection:

> *And such were some of you. But you were washed, but you were sanctified, but you were justified in the name of the Lord Jesus and by the Spirit of our God* (1 Corinthians 6:11).

Second, we currently are living out *actual holiness*. This is what we see in ourselves as we live on earth. We have a responsibility to constantly "put off the old self" and "put on the new self." We are hearing the voice of the Holy Spirit daily, and we yield to Him our habits, choices, attitudes, and will. We walk in humility before Him.

Important to note is that our careful obedience to the Holy Spirit and the lifestyle He directs, opens the door to hearing more from the Lord.

> *He replied, "You are permitted to understand the secrets of the Kingdom of Heaven, but others are not. To those who listen to my teaching, more understanding will be given, and they will have an abundance of knowledge. **But for those who are not listening, even what little understanding they have will be taken away from them**"* (Matthew 13:11-12 NLT).

I remember a time when I was ministering under the tents with my father. There was a period in which I wasn't seeing results the way I truly wanted. So I asked God to speak to me—to talk to me about how to operate more fruitfully. It seemed for days I was pleading with God to "Speak to me, Lord. Speak to me." After a few days, abruptly I heard, "I will speak to you again when you go back and do the last thing I told you to do."

I stood guilty...and convicted. God was showing me personally that when I choose to truly "listen," I will hear His voice more often and more clearly.

Holiness is about our character—our integrity. The world has had enough of believers in Christ who speak one thing with their mouths and live in a completely different way.

The walk of holiness is a walk of spiritually maturing, but it is a deliberate choice. It is a walk with the Spirit of God that allows His character to be developed in us. We don't participate in this walk to "earn" anything with God; but, on the other hand, there is a distinct "favor" upon those who have chosen this lifestyle of holiness. God honors those servants as sons and daughters.

The third phase of our walk of holiness is *final holiness*. This will come when all our striving ceases and we turn in this old earthly body for a new, glorified one.

> *Beloved, now we are the children of God; and* ***it has not yet been revealed what we shall be***, *but we know that when He is revealed, we shall be like Him, for we shall see Him as He is* (1 John 3:2).

What an amazing day we see ahead! How wonderful it will be to see Jesus and be exactly like Him, the Author and Finisher of our faith. In that day will be no more striving—we will live glorified and perfectly whole and holy—with Him!

FUNDAMENTAL KEYS

Dear reader, please especially remember these keys that open doors to increased anointing in your life: Holy Spirit empowerment; times of consecration with prayer and fasting; coveting the gifts of the Spirit with holy eagerness; and obeying the Spirit's voice when He tells you to move.

These keys will develop in you: Christ-like compassion for hurting people; familiarity with and authority in using the Word of God; childlike faith that will move mountains; and a growing spiritual perception that will develop you into an anointed, Spirit-led instrument in the hand of God.

Also remember the flow of the Spirit's work as you minister:

- Godly compassion leads us to the need.
- The eye of the Spirit reveals the important details of every need.
- The voice of the Spirit helps vocalize divine authority and bring total deliverance to hurting hearts and bodies.

Devour your Bible, pray often, set times of consecration, and covet the gifts. As you continue to learn the voice of the Holy Spirit and yield to His promptings, before too long you will be telling your own miracle stories.

Let's pray:

Father, I thank You for hungry hearts. I thank You that today we are living in the Church's finest hour. You have a full agenda for us, and we want to be ready. I ask You, by Your Spirit, to burn these truths into our hungry hearts. Reveal Yourself in new ways. Baptize us—immerse us—in the power of the Holy Spirit. Let our hearts be sensitive to Your voice and to Your ways. In this precious reader, Lord, grow a heart of obedience and boldness and let there be fruit that remains for Your kingdom. Let this person see an anointing for miracles operating in his or her life in the days ahead. In Jesus' mighty name, amen.

A WORD FROM DONNA'S MOTHER

Most of my life I have heard the stories Brother Schambach tells. Some of the miracles that you read, I have heard a hundred times! No matter how often I hear my husband tell them, they are always fresh. They demonstrate the miracle-working power of God.

Robert W. Schambach began his evangelistic ministry in 1955 while working with renowned evangelist A. A. Allen, from whom he received valuable training. This prepared him for the work to which God had called him.

In 1959, Brother Schambach began his ministry with a crusade in Newark, New Jersey, where signs and wonders followed. The revival lasted for six months! Reluctant to leave the new converts and friends, he founded a church, Newark Miracle Temple.

This pattern was repeated as Brother Schambach traveled across the East. Later on, other Miracle Temple churches were established in Philadelphia, Chicago, and Brooklyn. His reputation became that of one of the great "tent evangelists."

Across the country, Brother Schambach held great revivals under his ministry's tent, where virtually thousands of lost souls came to Christ. Thousands more received physical, financial, and emotional miracles. Brother Schambach's radio broadcasts and television programs soon became powerful extensions of the ministry with which God had blessed him.

Many of the miracles you read in this book took place while I was standing right beside Brother Schambach; I am an eyewitness to them. It is exciting to be there when God's power is at work. And, it is exciting to hear the miracle testimonies over and over again! I have watched little children sit spellbound with their eyes wide and their mouths open as Brother Schambach tells a story. I am sure you will agree, he has a unique and fascinating way of expressing himself.

I have also been privileged to see God formulate these lives that were supernaturally transformed into our extended family. God knit our hearts together in faith through the years, and I am blessed to be a part of such a family of faith and power.

I believe the miracle stories included in this book have elevated your faith. Use them as a reference of God's supernatural power when you need your faith renewed.

"Winn" Schambach
R. W. Schambach's wife, Winifred, of 61 years
September 3, 1926-April 20, 2010

A WORD FROM BROTHER SCHAMBACH

I BELIEVE IN MIRACLES!

If you cut all the miracles out of the Bible, you would not have a Bible left. It's a book of the miraculous, because our God is a miracle-working God. And my Bible declares that He is the same yesterday, today, and forever! You know what that means? It means He is still doing today what He did yesterday. He's still doing the miraculous! In fact, I believe we are going to see greater miracles in these last days than we have ever seen before.

Jesus began His public ministry as a ministry of miracles. Everything about His life involved miracles: His conception, birth, life, wisdom and teachings, ministry, death, resurrection, appearances, and ascension—all of these were astounding and undeniable miracles.

Jesus always attracted the multitudes by His miracles then, and He does so today, wherever miracles are done in His name. If we preach as the early Church preached, we will get the same results they received—miracles and healings. It doesn't matter where we are or who we are. If we want to get Bible results, we have to preach what the Bible says—miracles are part of the present-day ministry of Jesus Christ.

Some folks don't believe this. They say the days of miracles are over. You can even hear this from the pulpit. Some preachers say that the miraculous was only for the early Church. Many people have said that miracles were just for the days of the Old and New Testaments, but that is not true. God has not changed. He is the same yesterday, today, and forever. He is still in the miracle business. Jesus Christ is as much a miracle-worker now as He ever was, and people need His miracle touch now more than ever.

We are called to walk as the Christians did in the New Testament, to serve the needs of people today. Jesus must be allowed to live in us, in His power and with His personal presence guiding us.

When people act on God's Word in bold faith, the faith that produces miracles, then multitudes come from miles around, eager to see Christ's miracle power in demonstration.

The power of God is real today just like it was 2,000 years ago. I've seen hundreds of miracles with my own eyes—people being healed and set free by the power of the living Christ!

I get so many letters, phone calls, and emails from people who have received miracles from God. In my meetings, people come back to testify of how the Lord touched their lives. It blesses my heart to hear these stories of what God has done. I like to share them with the world, to let people know that God is not dead—He is alive and doing great things in all the earth. That is the reason for this book—to let the world know what the Lord has done.

Unfortunately, some Christians aren't aware of the power of God that is available to them as believers. A. J. Gordon, a theologian, once declared, "The Church is losing her grip on the supernatural." Too often all we see is a manifestation of the flesh and an emphasis on humankind's ability—what humans have learned.

Yet there is something crying out of every believer today, "I want to see a miracle! I want to see the supernatural!"

God is looking for every believer to take up his or her responsibility—to be obedient to His voice and help release God's miracle power. When we come to the place where we move on what God says, when He says it, miracles will become a way of life.

What do you have need of? You can pinpoint it. Maybe you need a healing in your body. Maybe your back is against the wall financially. Maybe you have a son who is hooked on drugs, bound by the devil, or a daughter who has run away from home. I don't care what the need is, God will perform a miracle in your life.

Your family may say you are crazy for believing God for a miracle. Your friends may look at you funny. Even your preacher may tell you that God doesn't work miracles anymore. Just let them talk. Let every one of them and let every devil be a liar, but let God be true! If He said it, He will do it! And if He spoke it, He will bring it to pass. No ifs, ands, buts, or maybes.

> *If you abide in Me, and My words abide in you, you will ask what you desire, and it shall be done for you. By this My Father is glorified, that you bear much fruit; so you will be My disciples. ...You did not choose Me, but I chose you and appointed you that you should go and bear fruit, and that your fruit should remain, that whatever you ask the Father in My name He may give you* (John 15:7-8,16).

Do you believe it? I'm telling you, friend, God's power works! If it didn't work, I would not have been in this for so long. I'd have done something else. But I cannot deny the power of God at work in the lives of people today.

Read this book over and over again. Let your faith come alive as you rehearse the Scripture and the testimonies. Then, as you begin to put the teaching into practice—get ready to receive your miracle!

R. W. Schambach
April 3, 1926-January 17, 2012

MORE MIRACLE TESTIMONIES

R. W. Schambach

A BLOOD TRANSFUSION FROM CALVARY

Dear reader, you may have loved ones who need a healing touch from God. Well, we preachers are no different. Sometimes we have great needs within our own families. Jonathan is the son of my niece, Joanne.

At age three, Jonathan was diagnosed with a blood disease—I.T.P. The platelets in his blood were being destroyed; and within a 24-hour period, there were black and blue bruises all over his body.

His parents didn't know what was happening to him so they took him to the doctor. This particular doctor, when he examined Jonathan, just blurted out, "Oh, your son has leukemia." This devastated Jonathan's parents.

It wasn't long before the boy was in the hospital and was put on heavy medication. They had to pad his crib because the disease caused him to bruise very easily.

It was during that time when I brought the big Gospel tent into that area of the Bronx, New York. One night we had a children's blessing service. My main emphasis that night was healing. And I'll never forget Jonathan's father, Pastor Mark Gregori, bringing him up to the front to be prayed for.

I took the boy from his father's arms and held him. Then I prayed over him, "Give him a blood transfusion from Calvary! In Jesus' name."

Within that same week, Jonathan's platelets came to the right level. The disease was gone! There were no more bruises. He was made completely whole!

Jonathan is a grown man now, and in 2010 God began using him as the Operations Manager of Schambach Ministries. His life is a miracle and his testimony is a marvelous example of God's healing power that is still at work today.

MIRACLE CANDY

One night in Philadelphia, a lady came to me and gave me some candy to wear. You can tell by looking at me that I like candy. So I accepted it and thanked her for it. She said, "That isn't for you."

"Well," I said, "you just gave it to me."

She said, "I want you to wear it."

I said, "Hold it, girl. I don't wear candy. I eat candy. What's wrong with you?"

She said, "Brother Schambach, you are going to wear that candy while you preach."

Did you ever run into a stubborn woman? There are a lot of women who will never take no for an answer—they are going to press through and get what God has promised them. This was one of those ladies. She said, "You are going to wear that candy."

I said, "No, I am not going to wear it, woman. What's wrong with you? Other preachers already talk about me wearing cloth. If they find out I'm wearing candy, my name is mud."

She said, "Brother 'Mud,' you are going to wear that candy."

She was very persistent. I said, "I am not going to wear it." I just withdrew myself from it. I said, "Why don't you make it a cloth like everybody else does? I will give you a cloth—take my hanky!"

"No, I don't want it," she said. "You are going to wear this candy. I have cloths from your office. I have them from Oral Roberts. I have them from T. L. Osborn. I have a sister in a mental institution. She has been there for thirty years. I send her cloths, but they censor her mail, and they know what those cloths are. The cloths end up in the wastebasket. I just came from there and they told me I can send candy to my sister. Now, you and I are going to put one over on the devil. We are going to cast him out with that candy."

I looked at her and said, "Give me the candy!" I put it in my left hip pocket and started preaching. I returned it to her at the end of the service. "You send it to your sister," I told her.

Six months later, I came back to that city, and I was preaching in the Metropolitan Opera House. I was receiving the offering that night when I saw two ladies come in. To be perfectly honest with you, I didn't remember the woman with the candy. She came walking down the aisle and dropped her offering in the basket and said, "Praise the Lord, Brother Schambach."

I said, "Praise the Lord."

She said, "This is my sister."

I said, "Hi, sister, glad to have you in church."

She said, "Brother Schambach, this is my sister."

So I dropped the bucket, got her by the hand, and said, "Welcome to our crusade." I didn't want to offend her.

She said, "Brother Schambach, do you remember who I am?"

I said, "No, ma'am, I'm sorry I don't."

She said, "I'm the one who gave you the candy!"

I stopped the offering collection and said, "Everybody go sit down. Forget the offering. I want to hear this."

I didn't get to preach that night. That woman tore the place apart. She told the story that I just told you. Then she said, "I sent that candy to the hospital, and the moment my sister bit into the candy, she bit into the power of God. The demons came out of her instantly, and she was in her right mind for the first time in thirty years."

The hospital staff didn't call the sister for about two weeks. Can you imagine that telephone call? "Come and get your sister."

"What do you mean, come and get her. Is she dead?"

"No! She isn't dead!"

"Well, what's wrong?"

"We don't know. All we know is that for the last two weeks, we have put her through a series of tests. She has been examined by every psychiatrist and every psychologist who had anything to do with her case. For the first time in thirty years, your sister is in her right mind."

What a miracle! This woman started attending a church in Philadelphia that used to be pastored by my brother-in-law, Reverend Harry Donald. She went on to live a normal life and was able to work because her sister didn't give up!

But the preacher almost cost her the miracle..."I am not going to wear that candy!" I learned my lesson that night!

A MIRACLE IN PROGRESS

Not every miracle happens instantaneously. Some miracles are progressive. They don't happen all at once.

I saw this firsthand in Canada, when I put my tent up on the Indian reservation in Hobbema, Alberta.

There was a 17-year-old teenager in the audience named Billie Dee Sharmon. The doctors had told her she had all kinds of sicknesses. She could barely move, and didn't attend school for three months. God delivered her from these infirmities at the tent service.

But there was one thing left that God had not healed, and she came back to the tent the next night ready to receive this final miracle.

When I had my testimony time before the message, she and her mother walked across the platform and told the people how God had healed her. I was thrilled to hear the testimony.

But before they left the platform, they had another request from God.

She had lost a lot of her vision because of the sickness. She was going blind. When she was healed, part of it had been restored. But she was believing God for all of it to be restored. They told me this right there on the platform. That's faith!

So I looked at them and said, "You don't have to wait for that. We can pray right now. Right here on television."

You see, I broadcasted this message on television. Some preachers might be nervous about everybody watching them pray for the sick. But I love to demonstrate the power of the Gospel. I like to show it, to put it on display!

I had my daughter, Donna, and another pastor join me to pray for her. We ganged up on the devil. I took the girl's glasses off and got ready to pray. But I only got one word out!

"Father—"

Immediately, I felt the power of God on that ramp. And so did she! As we had our hands on her, she just flopped like an old dishrag. It was the anointing of the Holy Ghost!

"Give her 20/20 vision! In the name of Jesus," I prayed.

I knew she wouldn't be able to talk in that state, so I had them take her off the platform.

A little later in the service, Donna came running up to me with the news that the young girl had clear vision! So we brought her back up to see what the Lord had done.

I did a little test to see how clear her vision was, and sure enough, her eyes were totally restored. She didn't need glasses anymore.

Hallelujah! It was a progressive miracle. God worked on her a little bit at a time, but He completed His work there in that anointing-charged atmosphere, right in front of the television cameras

MY BATTLE WITH THE DEVIL

I was on the turnpike, driving from Philadelphia to Chicago. I had plenty of time in the car. I was speaking in tongues, prophesying, and dancing. Have you ever danced while you were driving? It was just me and Jesus in that car. Just me and Jesus, having time together. No one was around to say, "You aren't in the Spirit." Just me and Jesus in that automobile.

I was halfway through Ohio, when all of a sudden a pain struck me in the fifth rib. I doubled over the steering wheel. At that moment, my foot hit the brake.

Ole Slewfoot was sitting on my shoulder. "Heart trouble," he whispered.

I wondered how he got in the car with all the tongue speaking, prophesying, and shouting. How did that devil get in here?

I pulled over to the shoulder of the road and engaged the devil in a conversation. He asked, "How many people did you bury this week?"

I was doubled over, but I thought of all the funerals I had preached at that week. "Four of them," I said.

"What did they die from?" he asked.

Every time that devil jumps on you, he knows how to mess your faith up—even while you are speaking in tongues. He said, "How many of your brothers have died?"

I said, "There's Ruben, Henry, Charles—four?"

"What did they die from?"

If I had seen a grave, I would have jumped in it. That's how bad it hurt! Then I came to my senses and said, "You filthy, rotten, lying devil. You are a liar. How can I have heart trouble when Jesus lives in there?"

He said, "Still hurts, doesn't it?"

I said, "Let it hurt. I am healed anyway. If God said I am healed, then I am; healing is mine."

I pulled the keys out of the ignition. I locked the car and said, "Slewfoot, wait here. I will be back. If I have heart trouble, I won't see you again. I am going to run down this turnpike, and I am going to jog until I get my second wind." I took off running—until I got my second wind. I felt so good as I was coming back that if I would have seen Mohammed Ali, I believe I could have whipped him right then.

When I got back to the car, I couldn't find the devil anywhere. I said, "Where are you, devil? Where are you? I want you to know, I am healed!"

But the devil was long gone. Only Jesus was there.

> *But He [Jesus] was wounded for our transgressions, He was bruised for our iniquities; the chastisement for our peace was upon Him, and by His stripes we are healed* (Isaiah 53:5).

IT'S NEVER TOO LATE

Some time ago, when I was in Seattle, Washington, I preached a message about Lazarus. The Bible says that Lazarus had been in the grave four days when Jesus finally came. Although it seemed as if He had arrived too late, He was right on time. He is never too late. In other words, it's never too late for a miracle.

Sometimes we put time limits on God. Mary and Martha were limited in their faith. They said to Jesus, "Lord, if You had been here, my brother would not have died" (John 11:21,32). They had forgotten that Jesus was Christ, the Son of God—Emmanuel: God with us. They had forgotten that Jesus is the Resurrection and the Life.

They didn't know that Jesus had intentionally waited. He wanted His followers to witness His miraculous power.

We should never try to figure out God's timetables. He is always on time. It's never too late.

After the service, a woman came to me and shoved a piece of paper into my hand. She said, "Now, I dare you to say it's not too late." Do you know what the paper was? A divorce paper, a final decree. She had just received it from the judge. It was final. The husband was gone. She looked me right in the eye and said again, "Now, I dare you to say it's not too late."

So I smiled and took her dare and said, "It's not too late."

She said, "What about that paper?"

I said, "You are looking at the wrong paper. My paper says, 'Therefore what God has joined together, let not man separate' (Matthew 19:6). That is what I believe. How long have you been married?" She told me they had been married for twenty-seven years and had five children. I said, "That man has no business leaving you." I laid hands on her and said, "Holy Ghost, bring that rascal to his senses and save him. Don't bring him back home the way he is. Lord, save him and fill him with the Holy Ghost." I looked at the woman and said, "Go home and get ready for your husband. He is coming."

Of course, that was easy for me to say. I was leaving town. I am an evangelist. I can hit them and run. But in all honesty, I believed what I had said. My wife and I drove from Seattle to Philadelphia. When we got to Philly, I had a letter, from that woman, waiting for me. I opened it, and the first lines said, "Dear Brother Schambach, God is never too late! God got a hold of that rascal, saved him, and filled him with the Holy Ghost. The Lord brought him back home, and we got married all over again."

That is the powerful aspect of faith. Take a stand of faith and say, "Devil, you are a liar. I am going to believe God for a miracle because He is going to turn this situation around." Speak faith. Speak to that mountain, and that mountain has to obey your words. That is how you will experience the power of faith.

TWENTY-SIX MIRACLES

When I was on the Phil Donahue show, he asked me, "What is the greatest miracle you have ever seen?"

Of course, I told him the greatest miracle is that Jesus reaches down into the depths of sin, picks up a person and washes that person in His blood, clothes him or her with His righteousness, and writes that person's name in the Lamb's Book of Life. That is the greatest miracle.

But what Phil wanted to know was what kind of healing or supernatural occurrence in the everyday world was the most dramatic move of God I have ever seen. And I have seen so many.

Oftentimes, I have seen miracles come as a result of a sacrificial offering. That doesn't mean we can buy a healing; but we can show faith with an offering, and God will take that faith and use it to meet our need. I'll never forget; the greatest miracle I ever witnessed began with an offering.

It happened under the ministry of Brother A. A. Allen. I was with this man of God for about five years in the 1950s. When this great miracle happened, Dr. John Douglas and Brother Allen were together. I believe it was one of the greatest evangelistic teams of that day.

A woman brought her child, who had twenty-six major diseases, to our meeting. I'll never forget this as long as I live. The boy was born blind, deaf, and mute. Both arms were crippled and deformed. His elbows protruded up into his little tummy; his knees touched his elbows. Both legs were crippled and deformed; he had club feet. When he was born, his doctors said that boy would never live to see his first birthday, but they were wrong; he was approaching four years of age.

Of course, his condition was breaking his mama's heart. She came to our meetings all week, and I got concerned about that boy. In those crusades, we had each person with a need fill out a prayer card, and as the Holy Spirit moved, we would pray for the needs God inspired us to pray for. And the Holy Spirit didn't seem to be moving us to pray for that little boy.

The following Sunday, his mother came to me and said, "Brother Schambach, I'm down to my last twenty dollars. I've paid the hotel bill, but we've been eating in the restaurant, coming to three services a day, and giving in every offering. All the money has run out. My baby has not been prayed for." She was very upset, and she was ready to go home.

I said, "Ma'am, I can't apologize for the moving of the Holy Ghost. I know you have to leave tonight, but if you come to the service and once again, the Holy Spirit leads in another direction, and your son's prayer card is not drawn for prayer, I will personally take your baby to the man of God's trailer house and see that he lays hands on your baby. You will not leave disappointed." And I meant that from my heart.

That night I came out, and I led the singing in that evening service. Then I introduced Brother A. A. Allen, and he came bouncing out on that platform and said, "Tonight we're going to receive an offering of faith." I had never heard him use that expression before, and I saw eyebrows lift all over the congregation. He went on, "Now, if you don't know what I mean when I say an 'offering of faith,' I mean for you to give God something you cannot afford to give. That's a good definition, isn't it? If you can afford it, there's no faith connected to it. So give Him something you can't afford to give."

As soon as Brother Allen said that, I saw that boy's mother leap out into the aisle and come running. Three thousand people were watching her in that Birmingham Fairgrounds Arena as she threw something in that bucket. I never saw anybody in such a hurry to give, and I confess, I was nosy. I came down off that platform to see what she had given. You know what I saw in that bucket? A twenty-dollar bill.

I knew that was all she had. She had told me that. She had driven from Knoxville, Tennessee, to the meeting in Birmingham, Alabama. She didn't know how she was going to get home or what she was going to use to feed herself and her baby on the way. I went behind the platform and wept. I prayed, "Lord, I've been trying to teach that woman faith all week. But now I'm asking You to give me faith like she's got!"

I don't know whether I could have done what she did, and you don't know if you could do it. We will never know, unless we are in a similar situation. But Brother Allen went on and collected the offering and launched into his sermon. But about fifteen minutes into his message he stopped and said, "I'm being carried away in the Spirit."

I said to myself, "Here we go again on another trip." This is how God used him: he said he could see what the Holy Spirit wanted to communicate to him like he was watching it on a television screen. He would describe it as he saw it. That night he said, "I'm being carried away to a huge white building. Oh, it's a hospital." Of course, I heard this kind of thing every night that I worked with Brother Allen, so I was sitting there unmoved.

Then he said, "I'm inside the hospital, and there's no doubt in my mind where I'm heading because I hear all these babies crying. It's a maternity ward. I see five doctors around a table. A little baby has been born. The baby was born with twelve, no, sixteen, no, twenty-six diseases."

When he said that, I started getting chill bumps up and down my spine. I said, "Oh, my God, tonight's that baby's night!"

Brother Allen continued, "Twenty-six diseases. The doctors said he'd never live to see his first birthday, but that's not so. That boy is approaching four. Now I see the mother packing a suitcase. They're going on a trip. Another lady's with her. The baby's in a bassinet. It's in the back seat of an old Ford. They're driving down the highway. I see the Alabama-Tennessee border. That automobile is driving in the parking lot. Lady, you're here tonight. Bring me that baby! God's going to give you twenty-six miracles."

The woman came running again for the second time that night. She put the baby in Brother Allen's arms. I jumped up to stand beside him, and everybody in the audience—3,000 strong— was standing. Brother Allen must have wanted to be sure that the audience was agreeing in faith for the miracle because he said, "Everybody close your eyes." But I thought, Not me, mister. I'm going to be scriptural on this one. I'm going to watch and pray. I've been waiting for this all week.

That little boy's tongue had been hanging out of his mouth all week. The first thing I saw as Brother Allen prayed was his tongue snap back into his mouth like a rubber band. For the first time in four years, the little guy's tongue was in his mouth. I saw two little whirlpools in his eyes, just a milky color. I couldn't tell whether he had blue or brown or what color of eyes. But during the prayer, the whirlpool ceased, and I saw two brand-new brown eyes! I knew God had opened his eyes, and if God opened the eyes, I knew He had opened his deaf ears.

Then his little arms began to snap like pieces of wood; and for the first time, they stretched out. His legs cracked like wood popping. All of a sudden, I saw God form toes out of the club feet as easily as a child forms something with silly-putty. The crowd was watching and by this time, going wild! I've never seen any people shout and rejoice so much in all my life.

I saw the baby placed on his feet, and he began to run for the first time in his life. He had never seen his mama before, never said a word, but he began running across the platform—and I was running right after him trying to catch him. He leaped into his mama's arms and I heard him say his first word, "Mama."

This miracle charged up the people of God so much that even more miracles began to happen there in Birmingham. We stayed for a week after that. People were bringing their handicapped friends and family members. There were about twelve or thirteen people in wheelchairs over against one wall on the left side of the platform, and about fifteen or so people who had been brought from the local hospital on stretchers on the right side of the platform. When everybody saw the power of God at work, all the handicapped people in wheelchairs stood up like a platoon of soldiers and walked out of there healed by the power of God, without hands ever being laid on them.

Then 3,000 pairs of eyes, like they were being conducted by a conductor, looked in anticipation from the wheelchairs to the stretchers and saw them get up and walk out of there healed by the power of God! Six blind people in the audience came running down the aisle with their white canes and threw them on the platform. Their eyes had been opened! Hearing aids began to pile up, then canes and crutches. Everybody in the building was healed.

It was an incredible time of miracles, and the power of God fell, starting with the twenty-six miracles for that one little boy. The following Saturday after his healing, I received a special delivery letter from his mother. She knew that I had a soft spot in my heart for her little son, so she wrote me. She said, "Brother Schambach, I took the baby to the hospital Monday morning, and the doctors won't give him back. They have kept him all week. They have called in every doctor from all across the country who has had anything to do with the case. They have pronounced my baby cured of twenty-six major diseases." Of course, we went on to get the copies of the affidavits from the doctors certifying that boy's life was a genuine miracle.

But there was a P.S. in that dear lady's letter, and a P.S. always means there's something more to the story. Her letter continued, "You remember that last Sunday when I told you all I had was twenty dollars? God knows that was the truth. But when that man of God said to give something you can't afford, I leaped into the aisle. The moment I hit the aisle, for the first time in my life, I heard the devil talk. The devil told me, 'You can't give that; that's not yours. Fifteen dollars of that goes to the doctor. Five dollars is for gas to get home.' The faster I ran, the faster he talked. But as soon as I turned loose of that money, he stopped talking. Ain't no use talking now. It's gone! It's been put in the bucket now.

"Brother Schambach, all you saw was those twenty-six miracles, but there is one you don't know anything about. After you were gone, people were staying there. They wanted to see the baby and see what God had done. People shook hands with me. When one lady shook my hands, I felt a folded piece of paper between our palms. I opened it up and saw it was a twenty-dollar bill. As I shook hands with the people who had lined up, every one of them had a folded paper in their hand. I went into the ladies room and counted $235!

"Isn't that just like God? He not only gave me 26 miracles for my baby, but He allowed me to stay in a hotel for a week, pay my bills, eat three meals a day in restaurants, give in three offerings every day, and still go home with more money than I came with!"

You can't beat God giving, no matter how much you try. Hallelujah! I believe with all my heart, as a result of what I saw, that the miracle had its origin in that gift of faith. When God dealt with that woman, she gave her last, and her last became her first.

COW MONEY

Years ago in Seattle, two tornadoes tore through and destroyed our tent. Now, it was the devil that caused this disaster. But God can take a disaster, turn it around, and work it for His glory.

We could not continue services in the tent, so I looked for a building. The Civic Auditorium was available over the next seventeen days. We didn't miss a meeting. And before we left town, enough money came in to buy a brand-new tent.

The devil just doesn't have any sense. The old tent that he destroyed was full of holes anyway. Now we had a brand-new one!

But it was a 12-year-old boy who started the whole thing.

I received the offering one night, and I happened to see a little boy walking down the aisle with a five-dollar bill in his hand. Tears were running down his face. You know how we human beings often make snap judgments and form first impressions? I thought, I wonder what that kid is crying for? His mama gave him that five dollars. Maybe he just didn't want to walk down with her with it.

He headed right for the bucket that I was holding. I said, "What are you crying for, boy?"

He threw the five dollars in the bucket and said, "Brother Schambach, that's my cow in there!"

I looked in the bucket and said, "Your what?"

I knew I had a story there, so I put the bucket in one of the pastor's hands. I took the little boy aside and said, "Tell me about it."

"I always wanted a cow of my own," he said. "But we lived in the city limits, and there's an ordinance that says you can't have cow in the backyard. But nine months ago, Dad moved out into the country. He called me and said I could have a cow now—but I had to pay for it. For nine months I've been saving my dimes. I've been running errands. I picked up a paper route. I get up at four in the morning and deliver newspapers. I've been saving five dollars for nine months."

I said, "Why are you putting that cow money in?"

He said, "I heard God's voice."

My God, that's the miracle to me! Giving five dollars is no miracle. But to see a 12-year-old boy obey the voice of the Lord that way! I asked him, "How did you know it was God?"

He said, "He called me by name. He said if I gave the cow money, He would give me the cow."

I looked at him and said, "Are you sure God told you that?"

"Yes, sir. He told me that."

I said, "Then dry up those tears! You're getting the best end of the deal!"

While the other folks were bringing their offerings, I sort of held onto his shoulder. I told all those people in that Civic Auditorium what I just told you about that boy.

Then a big, six-feet-seven, 270-pound man in bib overalls got up. He started crying. He walked up, and I said, "What are you crying for, brother?"

He said, "God just spoke to me."

I said, "What did God tell you?"

He said, "He told me to give that boy a cow."

I looked up and down at him. I learned this lesson a long time ago: the folks with the fancy suits don't have the money. It's the guys wearing the overalls. The guys with the suits on have all their money in the suits!

So I kind of did a double take on him and said, "Brother, do you have a cow?"

"I've got thousands of them, Brother Schambach," he replied. He was the biggest rancher in the state of Washington. When God told that boy to give, He already had a cow waiting!

The following Saturday this rancher had a Polaroid picture shot of the boy with his cow. He said to me, "Brother Schambach, I wish you could have been out at the ranch today. That boy came out with his daddy in a rented trailer to pick up his cow. I told him to go pick out any one he wanted. You know, that rascal picked the best one I had! And he never even thanked me for it. He just put his arm around that cow and raised the other arm up and said, 'Thank You, Jesus, for my cow!'"

He knew exactly who to thank—the cattle on a thousand hills belongs to God! (See Psalm 50:10.) God surely knows how to speak to a rancher to turn one of them loose.

After that little boy told his story, you should have seen how much money came in that offering. You don't have to beg people to give. You show them how God blesses and they'll want to get in on that blessing.

God was teaching that boy a principle—and teaching me a principle through that boy.

TITHING EGGS

When I was in Bible school, my wife and I would go out into the hills of Missouri every Sunday morning, and I would preach in a one-room schoolhouse. Farmers from all over that area would come. One precious lady, 83 years of age, would walk three miles, take her stockings off, and wade through a creek just to come and hear me preach. Even I wouldn't do that to hear me preach! (I was still learning how!)

She invited us to her home for dinner. She told us to park the car when we got to the creek and walk the rest of the way. We took our shoes off and waded through the creek, just like she did every Sunday. But that Sunday morning I was preaching on a difficult doctrinal subject—tithing. I said, "Ten cents out of every dollar you ever get hold of belongs to God."

There they sat with smiles on their faces—which I knew was the wrong reaction. I wasn't getting the message through to them. So I said it again, and still they smiled. Finally it dawned on me, you know why they're smiling? They don't have any money, and 10 percent of nothing is nothing! So I have to come at it from another way.

It's amazing what comes out of you when you're anointed. I said, "If you have ten cows, one of those cows belongs to God." All the smiles left.

I knew they understood it now.

I said, "If you have two hundred acres, twenty of them belong to God."

Nobody was smiling now.

After the service, a redheaded farmer came up to me, hands in his overall pockets. He said, "If my chickens lay one hundred eggs every day, does God get ten of the eggs?"

I said, "You got the message, brother. It's gratifying to know you got the message."

Without batting an eyelash, he looked me right in the eye and said, "You're not getting my eggs! The chickens aren't laying anyway!"

I said, "You know why those chickens aren't laying? Because you're robbing God! Those chickens can't even live a normal life!"

I didn't know how right I was. Remember, I was just learning. He looked at me and said,

"You mean to tell me if I give God what belongs to Him, those chickens will lay more eggs? Wait here!"

He got into the pickup truck and went back to the farm and brought a brown sack full of eggs. He laid them down at the altar. He came back to me, hands in his overalls, and said, "You going to be here next Sunday?"

I said, "Yes, sir."

He said, "This better work!"

I was so young in the Lord, I didn't know whether it was going to work or not. I went back to the Bible that week. I didn't get much studying done. But I got a whole lot of praying done. I was praying, "Lord, bless those chickens! Lord, give them a double portion! Let them lay double yolks, Lord!"

The next Sunday, my wife and I headed out to that little town. I said, "Honey, do you see anybody standing at the schoolhouse?"

She said, "I believe somebody's there."

I said, "Does the person have red hair?"

She said, "I'm not close enough to see that yet."

Sure enough, it was Red waiting for me. But I couldn't see his face. I didn't know whether he was mad or glad. I brought my old DeSoto to a halt and pulled on the emergency brake. Old Red came running to the car. I don't ever like to be at a disadvantage, so I jumped out of the car. He grabbed hold of me and started dancing me around the DeSoto.

"Preach, man, it worked, brother!" he cried. "Praise God, it worked! It worked!"

I breathed easy for the first time all week. Then I looked around and said, "Hold it, Red, wait! Where's the tithe?" I believed I had a right to ask him for that. I said, "If we made the thing work, where's the tithe?"

Hands still in his overalls, he said, "In there, at the altar, Preach. Brought 'em early today."

I walked into the one-room schoolhouse, and sitting in front of the altar was a whole crate of eggs—twenty-five dozen. I looked at him and said, "What did you do, bring them all?"

His hands were still in his overalls. "Just the tithe, Preach. Just the tithe." From a brown sack to twenty-five dozen!

He threw his arms around me and said, "Preacher, I ain't going to rob God no more."

I looked at him and said, "Me neither."

I believe we've all had an apple out of that bag. Then we wonder why we're not blessed.

God rewards obedience.

MULTIPLYING MONEY

I had a tent up over in East Saint Louis some years ago. I'll never forget a small woman—she was probably 68-70 years of age—who came to me. (I believe she must be with the Lord by now.) She said to me, "Brother Schambach, I want you to pray that God will let me rent a bus."

I thought, *What in the world would she want a bus for? That's the craziest request I've ever heard.* So I asked her why she wanted a bus. She said, "I want to take a crowd of people to hear Kathryn Kuhlman."

I said, "You want me to pray and ask God to give you money to get a bus so you can take a crowd of people out of my tent meeting to go hear a woman preach?" But I prayed. I asked God to bless her with it.

She said, "I already have $400, but I need a little over $800."

I took the paper sack of money she had, and I prayed. On Monday night she came back shouting. I never saw a woman shout like she did. She said, "Brother Schambach, I went home and counted the money that was in my bag—there was $500. I called my husband to count it because I thought I made a mistake. He sat down and counted it, and he got $600. I put it back into the bag, took it down to the bank the next morning and had the bankers count it. They counted $700."

The teller asked if she wanted to deposit it, but she didn't. She had the money put back into the bag. She took the bag down to the Greyhound Bus rental and said, "Here's my money for the bus." When they counted, there was a little over $800—enough to get her bus. She took a busload of people to hear Kathryn Kuhlman preach.

The Lord will provide! He will satisfy the hunger pains of the people. He rented a bus for a woman. I don't care what your need is; Jesus is a miracle-working God, and He will perform a miracle in your life!

What is your need? You know, people get into a rut many times, and they consider miracles only in the aspect of healing. But God is a miracle-working God in every phase of life!

THE MIRACLE OF GIVING

Give, and it will be given to you: good measure, pressed down, shaken together, and running over will be put into your bosom. For with the same measure that you use, it will be measured back to you (Luke 6:38).

Throughout the years I have learned an important truth—giving is a powerful tool for the miraculous.

God loves giving. It moves His heart. When we give, it is an expression of our total trust and obedience to God. Doors are opened in the supernatural realm when we give to God.

God wants to bless His people. He loves to pour out showers of blessing on those who serve Him. The testimonies that you are about to read will attest to that fact. Through these people's stories, you will see what the Lord can do through people who give to Him.

But listen to me. If we want the blessing of God in our lives, we must learn this principle: the blessing follows obedience.

> *"Will a man rob God? Yet you have robbed Me! But you say, 'In what way have we robbed You?' In tithes and offerings. You are cursed with a curse, for you have robbed Me, even this whole nation. Bring all the tithes into the storehouse, that there may be food in My house, and try Me now in this," says the Lord of hosts, "If I will not open for you the windows of heaven and pour out for you such blessing that there will not be room enough to receive it"* (Malachi 3:8-10).

Just imagine that. God wants to pour out a blessing on His people that's too big for them to receive!

But blessing only comes when we commit ourselves to obeying God by giving to Him. You cannot disobey God in the area of tithing without locking God's blessing out of your life. If you are a Christian, you should be going to the house of God weekly to worship, and you should pay your tithes there.

Too many individuals "worship" all week at the shopping mall shrines and pay more than tithes there. Then when they come to the house of God, they have nothing left to give. No wonder God's people are bound up with debt and financial difficulty.

You might say, "Brother Schambach, I would love to give to God, but I just don't have anything to give. I don't have any money."

Good! Since you don't have anything, you won't be able to take credit for it when God performs a miracle. He will get all the glory! God usually sends me to people who don't have anything. I have seen countless times how God has provided when there was a need, all because somebody stepped out in faith and planted a seed.

Listen, it's a biblical principle that when you step out in faith and plant, God will see to it that you reap a blessing.

God always has a miracle waiting for us if we'll just step out in faith and do what He's calling us to do. He will bless us beyond measure, not just financially, but in every other way, too. But He wants us to trust Him.

Now, anybody can trust Him when the checkbook is filled. But it takes faith to trust Him when the balance says "double zero." There's one thing that I've learned about God, though—He will make a way where there is no way.

If you are struggling in your finances, God wants to set you free. You do not have to be in bondage to debt or want. God wants you blessed. But you've got to step out on the water! You've got to let Him know that you mean business.

But this I say: He who sows sparingly will also reap sparingly, and he who sows bountifully will also reap bountifully. So let each one give as he purposes in his heart, not grudgingly or of necessity; for God loves a cheerful giver. And God is able to make all grace about toward you, that you, always having all sufficiency in all things, may have an abundance for every good work (2 Corinthians 9:6-8).

When you allow giving to be a way of life for you, it becomes a miracle tool in your hand.

Allow God to develop a giving heart in you. It may be hard at first, but God can help you to be a cheerful giver. Remember, you are not giving to man, who can sometimes be unthankful or careless. You are giving to God.

But now I want to pray for you. If you're struggling financially, agree with me now, and believe God to perform a miracle.

Father, I come to You in the name of Jesus. I bring this reader before You whose back is against the wall. I come against the bondage of debt in this person's life. Satan, you have no business in these pockets, so I command you right now to loose your hold on this person's finances. Lord, I pray that You develop in this individual a giving heart. And Lord, as this reader learns to give to You, I pray that You would open the windows of Heaven and pour out a blessing on this reader. Let it be above what he or she could even ask or think. Give my friend a testimony that will bring glory to You alone. In Jesus' name I pray. Amen and amen.

END-WORD

Evangelist Donna Schambach

Thank you, dear reader, for taking this marvelous journey with me.

As I relived these wondrous miracle stories from my father's legacy and from our expanding ministry, I was brought to tears again, I laughed again, I rejoiced again!

Most of all, I am so very grateful we have a mountain of evidence, that indeed *"Jesus Christ is the same yesterday, today, and forever"* (Hebrews 13:8 NLT).

Remember, as you have read what God has done in the lives of others, assured through their testimonies and the words of Scripture you read, you can exercise your own faith. And, YOU can be saved, healed, and set free by the power of the Risen Christ Jesus!

More than that, remember this—when God saves you, He saves you so that you can lead someone else to salvation. When He sets you free, He will use you to bring deliverance to others. You were chosen by God to function in the power of the Holy Spirit— with His heart of compassion, with His authority, in great faith and obedience.

I pray God gives you an increasing hunger for all of God's gifts—for His presence—for His wonder-working power. And, I pray, every day, you will see an increase of *The Anointing for Miracles* on your own life.

Please visit our website from time to time. I present a weekly podcast, Power Challenge, that is free to all, and it will continue to challenge your heart and encourage your faith. Write a letter of testimony and let me know how *The Anointing for Miracles* is operating in your life.

Also, stay involved with the ministry. God may lead you to take part in of one of our mission trips—or help us with our many mission projects. You will be able to partner in an ongoing way with a legacy of the supernatural that continues to impart to this generation.

DONNA SCHAMBACH

www.schambach.org

Schambach Ministries & Foundation

PO Box 9009

Tyler, TX 75711

Phone: 903-825-9361 (Prayer Line)

ABOUT THE AUTHORS

R. W. SCHAMBACH was a bold, powerful, Holy Ghost revival preacher. For more than 60 years, he conducted evangelistic crusades across the United States and around the world.

Brother Schambach's meetings were noted for enthusiastic worship, faith-building testimonies, and challenging, Bible-based sermons. His demonstrative preaching style and down-to-earth practical messages endeared him to thousands of people who found inspiration, encouragement, and deliverance in his services.

One of Brother Schambach's trademarks was the large Gospel tent used for so many city-wide and regional crusades. For many years, he took the "canvas cathedral" into inner-city locations where many preachers would not go, where he attracted many people who would have never attended a typical church service.

Despite graduating from seminary and having various degrees conferred upon him, he was known simply as "Brother Schambach" to those to whom he ministered. He had tremendous compassion for people, often praying for them one at a time long after his services had ended.

Brother Schambach personally conducted major open-air crusades and meetings in many countries worldwide, attracting some of the largest crowds ever assembled in the history of some nations. Brother Schambach also touched countless lives through television and radio ministry.

Robert W. Schambach passed away in 2012. He and his wife, Mary Winifred, had three children: Robert Jr., Donna, and Bruce; six grandchildren: Rachel, Trey, Jessica, Amanda, Christi, and Craig; and seven great-grandchildren: Brooklyn, Noah, Ellison, Royce, Mia, Eden, and Jaxson.

DONNA SCHAMBACH, only daughter of the late global evangelist, R. W. Schambach, has been an educator, lecturer, pastor, and evangelist. Her ministry began in New York City in 1983 and then broadened when she joined her father in 1991 as general manager, mission's coordinator, and team evangelist—traveling to more than 40 nations of the world to encourage pastors and leaders and plan mass evangelism outreaches.

For more than a decade, she also served as day speaker with her father under the historic Gospel tent, in the inner cities of the United States. Obeying her divine mandate to disciple, empower, and release believers from all nations, Donna conducts mass evangelism crusades, pastors and ministry leaders' conferences, as well as humanitarian outreaches around the world.

Still based in Tyler, Texas, Donna is the president of Schambach Ministries & Foundation. Whether in a church setting or on the mission field, Donna is known for bringing a powerful word of the Lord, often prophetic in nature; and, as Donna usually lays hands on the people, the Holy Spirit accompanies the ministry with signs following.

CONTACT INFORMATION

Schambach Ministries and Foundation
PO Box 9009
Tyler, TX 75711
Telephone: 903-825-9572
Website: www.schambachfoundation.org

A dedicated, faith-filled, Bible-believing prayer partner is ready to talk with you and pray about your needs. When you need prayer, call 903-825-9361. (If you cannot get through, leave your request and someone will return your call to pray with you.)

If you are a pastor interested in inviting Donna Schambach to minister at your service or conference, please send your letter of invitation to her by email to

keitel@schambach.org.